RESCUING WILDLIFE

RESCUING WILDLIFE

A Guide to Helping Injured and Orphaned Animals

PEGGY SUE HENTZ

STACKPOLE
BOOKS

Published by
STACKPOLE BOOKS
5067 Ritter Road
Mechanicsburg, PA 17055
www.stackpolebooks.com

Printed in the United States of America

10 9 8 7 6 5 4 3 2 1

First edition

Cover design by Tessa J. Sweigert

Photographs on pages 7, 45, 46, 47, 51, 64, 65, 85, 91, and 130 © Kathy Miller, www.CelticSunrise.com

Additional photographs by Peggy Sue Hentz, Lynn Dierwechter, Nadine Essick, Morrie Katz, and Andrew (Corky) Hanzok, Jr.

Library of Congress Cataloging-in-Publication Data
Hentz, Peggy Sue.
  Rescuing wildlife: a guide to helping injured and orphaned animals / Peggy Sue Hentz.—1st ed.
      p. cm.
  ISBN-13: 978-0-8117-3588-9
  ISBN-10: 0-8117-3588-5
  1. Wildlife rescue. I. Title.

QL83.2.H46 2009
639.9—dc22

2008049629

This book is dedicated to Dr. Jerry Bailey,
who spent his lifetime dedicated to saving animals
and lost his life doing the same.

Disclaimer

Personal contact with wildlife is accompanied by many dangers, including those that are mentioned throughout this book. The guidelines in this book are meant to help reduce these risks but cannot eliminate them. Instructions in this book neither imply nor promise absence of risk, and it is the reader's responsibility to use his or her best judgment in any actions undertaken.

Wildlife rehabilitation is regulated by both state and federal agencies. Regulations differ from one area to another and not all jurisdictions allow for the rehabilitation of all species. It is the reader's responsibility to learn and follow the laws pertaining to his or her locality.

The reader takes full responsibility for his or her actions and choices, whether or not the choice is to follow the guidelines and instructions set forth in this book. The author, publisher, and any and all agents involved in the production of this book shall not be held legally responsible for any consequences resulting from the reader's actions.

Contents

Acknowledgments

No rehabilitator can keep focused year after year on maintaining the welfare of wild animals and educating the public without a supportive partner. I am fortunate enough to have a life partner who not only believes in wildlife rehabilitation, but who also has become actively involved, taking on my mission as his own.

My first acknowledgment is therefore to Morrie Katz, who not only did all the proofreading of this book but also actively participates in rescuing animals, promoting Red Creek Wildlife Center, and teaching in our public education programs. Morrie is Red Creek's first certified Wildlife Capture and Transport Specialist, Red Creek's Public Relations Officer, my partner, and my best friend.

I would also like to acknowledge Red Creek's team of volunteers, who are essential to our continued success. Past and present, Red Creek has been blessed with dedicated, hard-working people who arrive daily to clean, feed, and tend to the animals in our care. Without them, I would never have time for anything besides taking care of the animals, and I would never have had the opportunity to write this book. My heartfelt thanks go out to the selfless students and adults who commit their time and energy to helping animals in distress.

My third thank you is an unusual one. It is to the person who started my journey in wildlife capture, which eventually resulted in the writing of this book. He is not a friend and never worked with Red Creek, and he was actually quite an annoyance for some time. He will go unnamed, but his actions started the ball rolling in wildlife capture and transportation becoming professionalized in Pennsylvania. In order to understand, I must tell you the story.

I had been rehabilitating wildlife for more than ten years, but Red Creek did not have a wildlife capture program. If I had the time, and the situation called for it, I would drive out to capture an animal in distress. For the most part, we relied on the public to bring the animals to us. Many hours were spent on the phone giving instructions about how to safely capture and transport animals—the same information you now hold in your hands.

The local man I mention bought an old, surplus ambulance and opened an animal rescue business. He had neither the authority nor the knowledge to pick up wild (or domestic) animals but had begun to do so regularly on his own.

To give you a better idea of this man's personality, consider the following: once, when a rehabilitator went to his home to retrieve a baby dove, the man entered the room in a full bio-containment suit. At other times, he was arrested and convicted for unlawful activities involving his service, and he was once ordered by a judge to have no further involvement with animal rescue.

Such is the story, but it did drive home an important point: there was no active wildlife capture program in the area. I decided, since we had a large, active volunteer base, we would work toward getting some of our staff licensed for wildlife capture. I contacted the Pennsylvania Game Commission for guidelines but was disappointed at the incomplete and outdated information they supplied.

I began to write new, more comprehensive guidelines for my staff. Those guidelines developed into two complete manuals: "Wildlife Capture and Transport," and "Critical Care—The First Twenty-Four Hours." The crux of the material involved determining when a wildlife emergency needs intervention versus normal wildlife behavior, which should not be interfered with. It also included descriptions of proper animal handling and how to return a baby animal, temporarily displaced, to its family.

The Pennsylvania Game Commission adopted the first of the two manuals as the new state guidelines and asked me to write a test based on that manual. Persons applying for a wildlife capture and transportation permit in Pennsylvania now receive that manual and test.

I also teach classes based on the material and have developed a dichotomous key for the public to use when faced with wildlife in distress. That key, the heart of this book, all started because of a surplus ambulance and a bio-containment suit.

Introduction

I t can happen quite unexpectedly on any given day. You are going about your business of work, family, and life, and suddenly a wild animal interrupts everything. It could be a baby bird on your porch or an injured squirrel in the street. It could be presented to you by a child or a pet. However it happens, this hapless creature becomes the center of your life for a short time and, if you care about animals (as I assume you do because you are reading this book), you want to do something—anything—to help.

The choices you make will have an impact on that animal's life and possibly your own. Having knowledge about the risks to the animal as well as to you, your family, and your pets, along with the right advice from the beginning, can mean the difference between an educational experience and disaster.

I am a licensed wildlife rehabilitator. I answer calls every day concerning foundling animals. The time it takes from the initial discovery until my phone rings can vary from moments to weeks, and that time often determines what we can (and cannot) do for the animal and the family involved.

During these calls, I often listen to the trials a person has gone through to find help: the numerous telephone calls with little or no guidance, the research that led to inaccurate information, and the attempts they made to care for the animal themselves. Many never knew that wildlife rehabilitators existed until someone pointed them my way.

In today's age of information, every subject can be researched on the Internet. Many people start their search for help there and end up following incorrect or incomplete advice on how to treat an injured animal or raise a baby animal themselves. They are often devastated when an animal dies or suffers because of failed attempts at helping it.

What they do not learn about are the many problems that may beset the animal even after an apparently "successful" release to the wild. Good nutrition and suitable husbandry along with the development of appropriate social behavior are essential to thriving in nature.

Not all of the information posted on the Internet is accurate, and one must be careful about the source from which information is gathered. If you come across a Web site that gives formulas or step-by-step directions on caring for a wild animal: *beware!* Professional organizations do not give out that kind of assistance, and the information provided is often wrong, deficient, and dangerous.

It's also a sad discovery when a person rescues a baby animal that didn't need help. The "rescue" itself may have been the only thing that put its life in peril. If the person finding the animal had immediate information at hand, he or she may have made better choices leading to freedom for the animal and enlightenment for the finder. Time is of the essence! Baby animals kidnapped for short periods of time can be successfully returned to the parent, den, or nest.

The purpose of this book is to supply you with accurate, immediate direction before you do anything dangerous or unnecessary. The recommendations contained in this guide will not only help you get the best possible care for the animal but will also have your safety in mind.

I've tried to present the information in an easy, orderly fashion so you can find exactly what you need to know when you need it. Although reading through the many chapters will help you understand the concepts behind wildlife rescue, the core of this book lies in the dichotomous keys beginning on page 1. Through a series of questions and answers, these charts will walk you through many common backyard wildlife scenarios and point you to the best information for your situation.

This book is not designed to be a step-by-step guide on how to rehabilitate wildlife or raise a baby animal. It is my firm belief that the science of rehabilitation should be left to licensed and trained individuals who have the knowledge, supplies, and veterinary support to offer that wild animal its very best chance. Although many people have successfully raised baby rabbits on homemade formulas, the future health and survival of all wild creatures depends on them having the best in nutrition, habitat enrichment, and reintroduction to the wild.

All states have laws governing the possession of some or all wildlife. These laws are in place to protect both the animals and the public. Wildlife rehabilitators are licensed by state and/or federal agencies and have the resources available to offer the very best to wildlife in distress.

Animals have not read our books on how they are supposed to behave. Every situation is different and poses unforeseen problems and dangers. To properly prepare in advance, I would strongly suggest you start by locating your closest wildlife rehabilitators and keeping their numbers at home, in your car, and in your cell phone.

If you are interested in working with wildlife, you might consider volunteering with your local rehabilitator or becoming one yourself. Again, the best place to start is with the licensed rehabilitator near you.

You can find resources for locating wildlife rehabilitators on page 124.

Chapter 1

DICHOTOMOUS KEYS

The dichotomous keys—or flow charts—for birds and mammals on the following pages are easy to follow. Directions are listed in the key itself, or for more thorough instructions, you will be directed to another section of the book. For this reason, it would be beneficial to have a bookmark on hand to mark your place.

We have tried to include as many common scenarios as possible, but no book can cover everything. Given the situation, you may need to speak directly with a rehabilitator or use your own judgment. Expect the unexpected. You are dealing with a wild animal, and unpredictability is the only firm rule.

Remember: keep your safety and the animal's safety foremost in your mind.

BIRDS

B1. Is this
   A. an adult? (GO TO B2)
   B. a nestling? (sparse or no feathers or covered with down) (GO TO B10)
   C. a fledgling? (has feathers but often the tail feathers are shorter than adult's) (GO TO B33)

B2. Has this bird been captured?
   A. Yes (GO TO B3)
   B. No (GO TO B4)
   C. It is trapped in a building (GO TO PAGE 42)

B3. Because of its ability to escape, an adult bird in hand is in distress and needs help. Be prepared to transport the bird to a wildlife rehabilitator.

- For more information on containment and transportation, please see pages 63 and 82.
- To find a rehabilitator near you, please go to page 124.

B4. Is the bird injured or sick? Are you sure?
   A. Yes (GO TO B5)
   B. No, but it's friendly and approaching people (GO TO B9)
   C. It is attacking my house, windows, or people (GO TO PAGE 116)
   D. I'm not sure. Help me decide (GO TO B8)

B5. Are you willing to safely capture and transport the bird to a rehabilitator?
   A. Yes (GO TO B6)
   B. No (GO TO B7)

B6. Thank you for being willing to go the extra mile for this animal. Please be prepared to transport the bird to a wildlife rehabilitator.

- For more information on safe capture, please see page 63.
- For more information on containment and transportation, please see page 82.
- To find a rehabilitator near you, please see page 124.

B7. Unfortunately, there is probably not much help available if you or someone else is not willing to get involved. Most rehabilitators are not in the position to be out capturing animals. Would you reconsider?
   A. Yes, give me the capture directions (GO TO B6)
   B. No

- To understand why these services are not commonly available, please see page 123.
- To locate a rehabilitator on the off chance they can arrange a capture and transport, please see page 124.

B8. The following are signs of a bird in distress (for more details, please see page 38):

> Bleeding
> Unconsciousness
> Abnormal use or position of limb(s)
> Odd head position
> Maggots
> Was in a cat's or dog's mouth
> Drainage from the eyes
> Behaving abnormally
> Cold and lethargic
> Heat exhaustion and exposure
> Inability to escape

    A. Yes, this bird is in distress (GO TO B5)
    B. No, it appears there is nothing wrong (GO TO B39)

B9. A friendly bird may be an imprint ("tame" from being hand-raised). This is often seen with waterfowl. It needs to be evaluated. Please contact a rehabilitator.

- To better understand imprinting, please see page 104.
- To find a rehabilitator, please see page 124.

B10. Is this baby bird sick, injured, or has it already suffered from extreme exposure (heat or cold)?
    A. Yes, help me locate a rehabilitator quickly! (GO TO PAGE 124)
    B. No (GO TO B11)

B11. What type of bird is it?
    A. Fishing bird (herons, egrets, loons, etc.) (GO TO B30)
    B. Raptor (GO TO B12)
    C. Waterfowl (ducks and geese) (GO TO B26)
    D. Songbird (small and helpless) (GO TO B31)
    E. Ground bird (pheasants and quail) (GO TO B26)
    F. I don't know. Help me decide (GO TO B35)

B12. Is this a hawk (also falcons), owl, or vulture?
   A. Hawk (also falcons) (GO TO B13)
   B. Owl (GO TO B16)
   C. Vulture (GO TO B21)
   D. I don't know. Help me decide (GO TO B25)

B13. What is the situation with this young hawk?
   A. Mother is known dead (GO TO PAGE 124)
   B. Nest fallen or nest removed (GO TO B14)
   C. In an inappropriate or dangerous location (GO TO B15)
   D. Alone but in a safe location (GO TO B15)

B14. Are the hawk's parents nearby?
   A. Yes (GO TO B17)
   B. No (GO TO B15)

B15. If the hawk's parents are in the area, leave it alone.

   Your definition of an inappropriate location may be different from the parents who chose this nesting site. Carefully consider the location and how you may be able to reunite the family. If you have seen the parents and you can safely do so, move the baby into a more secluded or safer place in that same area.

   A baby hawk in the middle of a busy street may be able to be moved to the surrounding forest.

   A baby hawk in the middle of an urban neighborhood may have fallen from a building. If it is not injured and you know the nesting area or the building, perhaps the bird can be returned to the nest. If the location is such that it is far too dangerous for the bird, and too dangerous for you to reach a safe area, then call a rehabilitator (GO TO PAGE 124).

   If you do attempt to reunite the family, monitor the baby for a few days. If it remains strong and healthy, the parents are caring for it. If it becomes weakened, then call a rehabilitator (GO TO PAGE 124).

B16. Owls come in a wide variety of sizes, and adults of small species are often mistaken for babies.

An adult owl will be fully feathered with no down. A baby owl will have thick down, while a fledgling owl will have both down and new feather growth.

Babies are typically born in the early to mid spring and fledge before summer. If it is any other time of year, please start over and consider this an adult owl.

Adult screech-owls, only six inches tall and the size of a softball, are often misidentified as baby great horned owls. Please compare the two pictures below to identify this owl.

A. This is a baby owl (GO TO B18)

Baby great horned owl

B. This is a small adult owl (RETURN TO B1)

Adult screech-owls

B17. Monitor the baby for a few days. If it remains strong and healthy, the parents are caring for it. If it becomes weakened, then call a rehabilitator (GO TO PAGE 124).

B18. What is the situation with this young owl?
  A. Parents are known dead (GO TO PAGE 124)
  B. Nest fallen or nest removed (GO TO B19)
  C. Inappropriate location (GO TO B20)
  D. On ground alone (GO TO B20)

B19. If the parents are in the area, leave it alone. Owls often leave the nest very early; therefore, it's natural for parents to tend to baby owls on the ground.

    If this is a small species of owl that may easily fall to predation, you can place the baby high up in a tree for protection.

    If this is a larger species, such as a great horned owl, and the baby has developed past a helpless hatchling, leave it where it is. It can defend itself from most predators.

    Monitor the family for a few days to make sure the parents don't abandon the baby because of the nest accident. If it remains strong and healthy, the parents are caring for it. If it becomes weakened, then call a rehabilitator (GO TO PAGE 124).

B20. Large owls, such as the great horned owl, leave the nest weeks before they can fly. The parents continue tending to them. Once they begin to develop feathers, they are able to defend themselves against common predators such as cats. Large dogs, however, may pose a threat. If they are still down-covered, they may not have yet developed enough to protect themselves and should be moved up into a nearby tree.

    Smaller species of owls, such as screech-owls, cannot defend themselves and, if they cannot yet fly, should be placed up in a tree out of harm's way.

    Some species, such as the short-eared and snowy owls, nest directly on the ground.

    Your definition of an inappropriate location may be different from the parents who chose this nesting site. Carefully con-

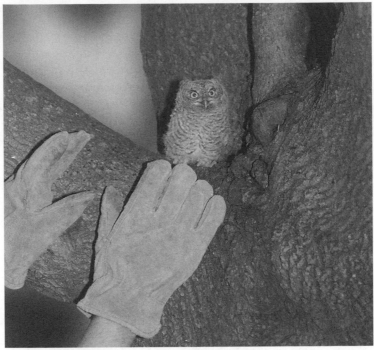

A nestling screech-owl is placed up in a tree.

sider the location and how you may be able to reunite the family. Usually, baby owls should be just left alone.

If you haven't seen the parents and you can safely do so, move the baby into a more secluded or safer place in that same area.

A baby owl in the middle of a busy street may be able to be moved to the surrounding forest.

A baby owl in the middle of a busy urban neighborhood is in grave danger. If it is not injured and you know the nesting area (probably a local group of conifer trees), perhaps the bird can be returned to the nesting area. If the location is such that it is far too dangerous for the bird, call a rehabilitator.

Monitor the owlet for a few days. If it remains strong and healthy, the parents are caring for it. If it becomes weakened, call a rehabilitator (GO TO PAGE 124).

B21. People often mistake baby pigeons for baby vultures. Here's how to tell the difference:

A. Pigeons are the size of a softball or smaller and have sparse down that looks like it was burned (GO TO B22).

Baby pigeons

B. Vultures have thick reddish or white down. Turkey Vultures have a "peep sight" at the nares (nostrils) (GO TO B23).

A baby vulture

B22. Pigeons nest just about anywhere. There are usually two babies, and there might not be a nest at all. They can be found on ledges, in old nests, and even on the ground under a bush. Mothers do not tend to them often, feeding only two to four times a day. If the baby is not injured, leave it alone.

B23. Vultures do not build nests and babies are often found alone on rock ledges, in caves, and even in barns and silos. This is natural. A baby vulture found in someone's backyard or hopping down the street is not normal and needs help (GO TO PAGE 124).

B24. If the babies can be captured, place them in a tall, slim box (like one an upright vacuum cleaner would come in) and set the box near the parents. Watch from a distance. The sound of the babies should attract the parents. Often the mother will come and knock over the box and take the babies with her. If she doesn't respond, the babies are already contained and you can take them to a rehabilitator.

• To find a rehabilitator, please see page 124.

B25. All baby raptors are covered with a thick down. Use this guide to identify your bird:

A. Hawks (also falcons) have curved beaks and strong feet that are completely bare (GO TO B13).

American kestrel

B. Owls have curved beaks and strong feet that are completely covered in down (GO TO B16).

Screech-owls

C. Vultures have thick reddish or white down. Turkey Vultures have a "peep sight" at the nares (nostrils) (GO TO B23).

Vulture

D. Baby pigeons are often confused with raptors (GO TO B22).

Pigeons

E. Grouse and chickens are often confused with raptors (GO TO B26).

B26. What is the situation with the waterfowl or ground bird?
   A. Mother is known dead (GO TO PAGE 124)
   B. Alone with no parent (GO TO B27)
   C. Babies are trapped in drain or other obstacle (GO TO B29)

B27. Do you know the location of the mother?
   A. Yes (GO TO B24)
   B. No (GO TO B28)

B28. Baby ducks, geese, and ground birds—such as pheasant, quail, and turkey—need their parents at all times. They are *never* left alone by the parents. Please take this baby to a wildlife rehabilitator who can raise it or who might be able to introduce it to a surrogate family of the same species.

   • To find a rehabilitator, please see page 124

B29. Each situation is different and beyond this key. As a general guide:
   If the mother can be captured, her calls will attract the babies toward a net, box, or corral.
   If the babies can be captured, place them in a tall, slim box (like one an upright vacuum cleaner would come in) and set the box near the parents. Watch from a distance.
   The sound of the babies should attract the parents. Often the mother will come and knock over the box and take the babies with her. If she doesn't respond, the babies are already contained and you can take them to a rehabilitator.

   • To find a rehabilitator, please see page 124

B30. *Danger*—**Please read the section on fishing birds (page 70) *before* approaching any babies or adults.**
   Because herons and egrets build their nests so very high up in the trees, returning a baby to its nest is nearly impossible. Nests are guarded almost all the time until the babies are about a month old.
   If the baby has feathers and appears otherwise healthy and uninjured, monitor the baby for a few days. If it remains strong

and healthy, the parents are caring for it. If it becomes weakened, call a rehabilitator.

If the baby is very young with down, it probably should be taken directly to a rehabilitator.

- To find a rehabilitator, please see page 124

B31. What is the situation with this baby songbird?
   A. Mother is known dead (GO TO PAGE 124)
   B. Nest fallen or nest removed. Tree cut down (GO TO B32)
   C. On ground. Out of nest. Inappropriate location (GO TO B34)
   D. Note on mourning doves: does your baby look like this? (GO TO B37)

B32. You can make a new nest for the baby bird, and the parents should begin caring for it again.

- For instructions on returning babies to nests or how to rebuild nests, please see page 44.
- To find a rehabilitator, please see page 124.

B33. Is this bird injured? Are you sure? Flightlessness doesn't always mean a bird is injured.
   A. Yes, this bird is injured (GO TO PAGE 124)
   B. I'm not sure if it's injured or not. Help me decide (GO TO B38)
   C. It is hopping around but can't fly (GO TO B36)

B34. If the baby bird is not injured, has not suffered from exposure, and you know where the nest is (and can reach it), place the baby back in the nest. *It is a fallacy that touching a wild baby will cause the mother to reject or kill it.*

    A. If the baby has suffered dehydration, is cold and lethargic, or has been exposed to the sun and is too hot, it needs to see a rehabilitator immediately (GO TO PAGE 124).

    B. If you know generally where the baby came from but cannot find or reach the actual nest, go to page 44.

    C. To locate a rehabilitator now, just in case, go to page 124.

B35. Which best fits this bird?

    A. Thick down with a curved, sharp beak and strong feet (GO TO B25)

    B. Thick down, can walk on its own, webbed feet (GO TO B26)

    C. Thick down, can walk on its own, slim toes (GO TO B26)

    D. Naked or sparse down, helpless. Might open its mouth begging for food (GO TO B31)

B36. Fledglings go through a period when they are just learning to fly. Depending on the species, it can take several hours or several days for them to get off the ground. Once they learn to fly, the parents gather them together and begin teaching them the survival skills they need, such as how to find food.

People often find fledgling birds temporarily stranded in a yard or on a porch and think they need help. Unable to fly, they become prey to pet dogs and cats.

This is an important transition time for these birds and should not be interrupted. Birds brought to rehab at this age often fail. They are not old enough to feed themselves, but they know we are not their parents and subsequently resist hand-feeding. Force-feeding places them under great stress and they will often die.

If they are uninjured, stranded fledglings can be moved to a safer location nearby. Moving them to a nearby tree limb or herding them to a safer area is all the "rescuing" they need.

B37. Mourning doves do not build elaborate nests. They often nest directly on the ground under a low bush. They will also nest in old bird nests, flower pots—just about anywhere. There are usually two babies to a nest.

Unlike other songbirds, the parents do not feed them often, but may only visit them for feeding several times each day.

It is easy to determine if a nestling dove has been recently fed by the parents. In the picture below, the dove on the right has been recently fed and has a swollen neck area. The dove on the left has an empty crop. A baby dove can be checked periodically to see if the crop area enlarges. If it does, the parents are feeding it.

If a baby dove is not injured, then leave it alone. It is fine and the parents are caring for it. *It is a fallacy that touching a wild baby will cause the mother to reject or kill it.*

Young fledgling and pre-fledgling doves look much like the adults. You can easily tell the difference by the shape of the tail. Adults have a sharply pointed tail, whereas a juvenile's is rounded.

Young doves are easily approached and should be left alone except when they have an obvious injury.

B38. The following are signs of a bird in distress (for more details please see page 38):

> Bleeding
> Unconsciousness
> Abnormal use or position of limb(s)
> Odd head position
> Maggots
> Was in a cat's or dog's mouth
> Drainage from the eyes
> Behaving abnormally
> Cold and lethargic
> Heat exhaustion and exposure

A. Yes, this bird is in distress

- To find a rehabilitator, please see page 124.

B. No, it appears there is nothing wrong. (GO TO B36)

B39. It appears nothing is wrong, but you may wish to monitor the situation for a day or so.

MAMMALS

Before we begin the mammal section, let's make sure there are no people in danger of exposure to rabies.

M1. Was anyone bitten or scratched, or did saliva from the animal come in contact with an open cut or mucous membrane such as the eyes? Have you been caring for this animal for a day or more, feeding it or handling dishes?
A. No (GO TO M3)
B. Yes (GO TO M2)
C. Rabies does not exist in this area (GO TO M3)

- For more information on rabies, go to page 100.

M2. Although any warm-blooded animal can contract rabies, some species (such as raccoons, skunks, and bats) are more prone to transmitting the virus.

  A. If you (or someone else) have had a possible exposure, call your family physician, hospital emergency room, or your state's department of health for information on your health and how to proceed.

- For more information on rabies, go to page 100.

  B. Continue with the mammal section (GO TO M3).

M3. Is this

  A. an adult? (GO TO M4)

  B. a juvenile? (eyes open but still dependant on parents) (GO TO M19)

  C. an infant? (eyes closed, unable to walk) (GO TO M11)

M4. What is the situation with this adult mammal?

  A. Animal is sick or injured but we have not captured it (GO TO M5)

  B. Animal is sick or injured and we have captured it (GO TO PAGE 82)

  C. Animal is acting friendly (or aggressive) and is approaching people or pets (GO TO M10)

  D. Animal is acting abnormally or "hanging out" (nocturnal animal out during the day) (GO TO M9)

  E. I am not sure if it's injured. Help me decide (GO TO M8)

  F. Animal is a nuisance and I want it removed (GO TO PAGE 114)

M5. Most rehabilitators are volunteers and do not have the ability to go out and capture animals. Are you willing to safely capture and transport the animal to a rehabilitator?

  A. Yes. Give me instructions for safe capture (GO TO M6)

  B. No (GO TO M7)

  C. This animal is too dangerous because of its size or aggressive behavior (GO TO PAGE 124)

M6. Only attempt to capture the animal if you can safely do so.

   A. For more information on specific capture instructions, please read "Injured Wildlife 101" on page 26 and "Capture" on page 63.

   B. To find a rehabilitator, please see page 124

M7. Unfortunately, there is probably not much help available if you or someone else is not willing to get involved. Would you reconsider?

   A. Yes, give me the capture directions (GO TO M6)

   B. No

- To understand why these services are not commonly available, please see page 123

- To find a rehabilitator, please see page 124.

M8. The following are signs of an animal in distress (for more details, please see page 38):

   Bleeding
   Unconsciousness
   Abnormal use or position of limb(s)
   Odd head position
   Maggots
   Was in a cat's or dog's mouth
   Drainage from the eyes
   Behaving abnormally
   Cold and lethargic
   Heat exhaustion and exposure
   Inability to escape

   A. Yes, the animal is in distress (GO TO M5)

   B. No, the animal is not in distress (GO TO M32)

M9. A nocturnal animal out during the day may or may not be a problem. If a mother has babies in the den, she may be hunting. Animals can also be routed from their den accidentally and become disoriented until they find a new place.

If the animal does not appear injured, give it a day or two for reorientation. The problem may rectify itself naturally.

- To find a rehabilitator, please see page 124.

M10. This is a very dangerous situation and can have many causes, including head injury, imprinting, or disease.

Unusual aggression or friendliness are two of the clinical signs of rabies. Even if not rabid, the animal should be treated as such. Do not take chances with your life.

Imprinted animals are those who were hand-raised (usually by the public) and have no fear of people. They are still wild animals, though, and even friendly ones can have a sudden change in behavior.

Do not approach this animal. Keep pets and children away. Call a rehabilitator immediately.

- For more on imprinting, see page 104.
- For more on rabies, see page 100.
- To find a rehabilitator, please see page 124.

M11. Is this infant animal sick, injured, or has it already suffered from extreme exposure (heat or cold)?
A. No (GO TO M12)
B. Yes. Help me locate a rehabilitator quickly!

- To find a rehabilitator, please see page 124.

M12. It is often difficult to determine whether a baby animal needs help, should simply be left alone to be whisked away by a parent, or just moved to a safer place. No one can raise a wild baby better than the parent. Great care must be taken in deciding whether or not to interfere.
A. Deer or fawn (GO TO M23)
B. Cottontail rabbit (GO TO M13)
C. Opossum (GO TO PAGE 56)
D. Other infant species (GO TO M24)

M13. What is the problem with this rabbit?
   A. Possibly abandoned or orphaned (GO TO PAGE 48)
   B. Baby not in nest and location of nest is unknown (GO TO PAGE 124)
   C. Nest was moved or destroyed by construction, gardening, etc. (GO TO M18)
   D. Lawn mower accident (GO TO M17)
   E. Brought home by children (GO TO M14)
   F. Nest in a public area and known to many children (GO TO M16)
   G. Brought home by pet (GO TO M15)
   H. Nest was discovered or touched (GO TO M14)

M14. Baby rabbits can be returned to the nest if these criteria are met:

   1. Babies are uninjured
   2. You have not possessed them more than one day
   3. You have not fed them any type of milk replacers, formulas, or other types of food
   4. You know the location of the nest

   It is a fallacy that touching a wild baby will cause the mother to reject or kill it.

   A. We do not meet these criteria. Please help me find a rehabilitator (GO TO PAGE 124).
   B. We meet these criteria. Please give the instructions for proper reintroduction to the nest and how to test if the mother returns (GO TO PAGE 48).

M15. Dogs, and especially cats, carry the bacteria *Pasteurella* in their mouths, which is highly infectious to wild animals, especially birds and small mammals such as squirrels and rabbits. If the animal was attacked or carried by a pet it will need a regimen of antibiotics to prevent infection.

   Any baby animal that was in a cat's or dog's mouth should be taken to a wildlife rehabilitator.

   • To find a rehabilitator, please see page 124.

M16. People and pets should be kept away from the nest for ten to fourteen days. If this is impossible or if you have no control over the property, take the babies to a wildlife rehabilitator right away.

It is a fallacy that touching a wild baby will cause the mother to reject or kill it.

A. If children or pets can be kept away, go to M14

B. If children or pets cannot be kept away, find a rehabilitator (see page 124).

M17. If some babies were injured or killed but others are untouched, blood from the injured babies will probably attract flies. These flies will lay eggs, and the hatching maggots will consume all of the babies. All babies should be taken to a rehabilitator.

If all the babies are unharmed, rebuild the nest and test to make sure the mother returns.

It is a fallacy that touching a wild baby will cause the mother to reject or kill it.

A. For instructions on testing the nest for the mother's return, go to page 51.

• To find a rehabilitator, please see page 124.

M18. Heavy construction often will cause abandonment of the nesting area. Gardening or accidentally disturbing the nest may not. Can the nest be rebuilt in the exact same location?

A. No (GO TO PAGE 124)

B. Yes (GO TO PAGE 51)

M19. Is this young animal sick or injured?

A. Yes, this animal is injured (GO TO PAGE 124)

B. No (GO TO M20)

C. I'm not sure if it's injured or not. Help me decide (GO TO M21)

M20. It is often not easy to determine whether a baby animal needs your help, simply left alone to be whisked away by a parent, or just moved to a safer place. No one can raise a wild baby better than the parent, so great care must be taken in deciding whether or not to interfere in that life.

   A. Deer (GO TO M23)

   B. Cottontail rabbit (GO TO M22)

   C. Opossum (GO TO PAGE 56)

   D. Other juvenile species (GO TO M24)

M21. The following are signs of a baby mammal in distress (for more details, please see page 38):

> Bleeding
> Unconsciousness
> Abnormal use or position of limb(s)
> Odd head position
> Maggots
> Was in a cat's or dog's mouth
> Drainage from the eyes
> Behaving abnormally
> Cold and lethargic
> Heat exhaustion and exposure

   A. Yes, the animal is in distress (GO TO PAGE 124)

   B. No (GO TO M20)

M22. Is this rabbit over four inches long, hopping, and able to make its ears stand up?

   A. No, this rabbit is younger than that (GO TO M13).

   B. Yes, that describes this rabbit (GO TO PAGE 48).

   C. This rabbit is over four inches but is in an unsafe location (GO TO PAGE 51).

Use a dollar bill, which is six inches long, to measure the rabbit.

M23. People often find fawns and think they have been orphaned or abandoned. The fawn will be seen day after day, in the exact same place, alone.

Was this fawn found with its dead mother or has it been alone in an area?

A. This fawn is approaching people and crying loudly for the entire day (GO TO PAGE 124).

B. This fawn is a true orphan found with the dead mother (GO TO PAGE 124).

C. There is no mother in the area. The fawn is alone (GO TO PAGE 52).

M24. What is the situation?

A. Found alone (GO TO M29)

B. Nest disturbed/animals touched (GO TO M26)

C. Mother is known dead (GO TO PAGE 124)

D. Nest destroyed/tree cut down (GO TO M25)

E. Exposed to the elements (GO TO M28)

M25. Place the babies under shelter and leave them alone in the area for a few hours (nocturnal animals may need to be left for the night). There is a very good chance the mother will return to retrieve them. Check back in a few hours. If they have not moved, call a rehabilitator.

- To find a rehabilitator, please see page 124.

M26. It is commonly believed that touching a baby animal will cause the mother to reject or kill it. This is not true.

Babies can be returned to the nest if these criteria are met:

1. Babies are uninjured
2. You have not possessed them for more than one day
3. You have not fed them any type of milk replacers, formulas, or other types of food
4. You know the location of the nest

A. We meet these criteria (GO TO M31)
B. We do not meet these criteria. Please help me find a rehabilitator.

- To find a rehabilitator, please see page 124.

M27. Do you know the location of the den or nest?
A. Yes (GO TO M31)
B. No (GO TO M25)

M28. Has the baby's health been compromised because of exposure? (Too hot or too cold?)
A. Yes (GO TO PAGE 124)
B. No (GO TO M27)

M29. Is the baby sick or injured? Is "being alone" its only problem? It is normal to find a healthy baby with no sign of the parents. They may be out searching for food or even watching from a distance. Some animals do not utilize dens, and babies can be found out in the open.
A. I don't know if it's injured (GO TO M30)
B. It does not appear injured (GO TO M26)
C. It is injured (GO TO PAGE 124)

M30. The following are signs of a baby mammal in distress (for more details, please see page 38):

Bleeding
Unconsciousness
Abnormal use or position of limb(s)
Odd head position
Maggots
Was in a cat's or dog's mouth
Drainage from the eyes
Behaving abnormally
Cold and lethargic
Heat exhaustion and exposure

A. Yes, the animal is in distress (GO TO PAGE 124)
B. No (GO TO M29)

M31. Please return the babies to their den.

M32. It appears nothing is wrong, but you may wish to monitor the situation for a day or so.

Chapter 2
INJURED WILDLIFE 101

The initial encounter with an injured animal can be heartbreaking. Human instinct tells us to help at all cost, but the results of a sudden, unplanned action can be very damaging for the animal and for you.

Stop, look around, and plan every action beforehand. If there are other people around, talk to them and work together. Create a plan and move from there.

Before taking any action, call for advice if you can. This is where having your local wildlife rehabilitator's number saved in your cell phone comes in handy. Keep a safe distance from the animal and relay any details you can about the species, size, and type of injury. Remember the location and the surrounding scene. Also describe any obvious injuries that you observe.

> If you need to capture the animal, think *safety* first: your safety as well as the animal's safety.

Forget about the kamikaze-style of animal capture where a person rushes in with reckless abandon as is often seen on television today. Such high-action scenes are probably well planned out before the camera starts rolling, and the drama is for ratings, not conservation.

Take a step back and review the situation carefully. As you scan the area, take a look at the animal before approaching it. In some cases, binoculars can be used to examine the animal before entering its danger zone.

Taking a short time to assess the situation and examine the animal before approaching it eliminates surprises and unnecessary injury to you, any bystanders, and the animal. Look for anything that can give clues to what happened. Seek out escape routes the animal may take and the dangers that await them there such as traffic, dogs, cliffs, and water.

PURSUIT

Animals that are difficult to approach can often be chased to an enclosed area such as a fenced yard, barn, or barnyard. Bystanders can help direct an animal to a confined location, thus trapping the animal.

On the other hand, pursuing an animal that is fleeing from you is not always a good idea. It is highly unlikely that you will be able to outrun the animal, and you could be seriously injured if you trip or fall. As humans, we are considered the most intelligent of species and you must "outthink" the animal so that you can capture it before it has a chance to escape. This is why surveying the area and having a capture plan is so important.

If an animal has escaped, and it is obvious that capture attempts will be futile, *stop*! If the animal can't be captured, it may not need help. Keep an eye out for the animal for several days. If its condition deteriorates, capture may be attempted later.

Before doing anything, ask yourself if you are truly prepared to help this animal.

Is it dangerous? Do you have the mobility and strength to control it without getting hurt?

Do you have a box, carrier, or other container in which to confine it? Do you have safety equipment such as gloves and eye protection?

Injured adult animals can present themselves in varying degrees of distress: from slightly injured and trying to escape, to self-defending, to completely unaware and possibly unconscious. Do not allow an animal's lack of response cause you to let down your guard. An animal can awaken suddenly and strike out. Many species will feign sleep as a way of protecting themselves. No matter what the degree of injury, treat the animal as if it is the most dangerous creature on the planet.

Helping Each Other

A female barn owl had found a wonderful spot to nest: a large ventilation fan thirty feet off the ground in the wall of a large barn. The area was quiet and secluded, and the soon-to-be-a mother owl laid seven perfect eggs.

But the area did not stay quiet long. While the mother barn owl sat incubating her eggs, a flock of chickens arrived at this commercial poultry farm. Suddenly, the large fan turned on and the mother owl's world turned upside down.

The woman farmer found the owl lying on the ground, unable to fly. Both wings appeared injured, and the mother owl was not responding. She called the Pennsylvania Game Commission, who delivered the bird, along with the seven eggs, to Red Creek Wildlife Center.

Doctor Lee Simpson, a certified avian veterinarian, was Red Creek's attending veterinarian at that time. She had recently studied new techniques in avian orthopedics and applied her new knowledge to the injured owl. Pins were placed inside three fractured bones, allowing the wings to heal.

As the owl recovered at Red Creek, her demeanor and personality (that of an extremely aggressive wild animal) returned. Wanting nothing to do with her caregivers, the owl would warn anyone nearby with a loud, raucous scream. Unheeded, the warning would be followed by an attempt to talon anyone whose task it was to feed the patient or clean her cage. The scream was deafening and reminded me of the old Japanese dinosaur movies I watched as a child. I named the mother owl "Godzilla."

Several weeks later the pins were removed and, although the wings appeared structurally perfect, Godzilla never attempted to fly. Her eggs had not survived the ordeal and were no longer viable. They were removed from the incubator and discarded. This lonely would-be mother owl was miserable; although we had saved the bird's life, we doubted she would ever regain her freedom.

One morning, another farmer came upon a devastating scene. Being environmentally minded, he had rejected the use of poisons and cats for rodent control and instead encouraged barn owls to nest inside his buildings. A family of barn owls had lived there for decades and was cherished by the farmer. That morning, he found the entire family on the floor of the barn. Two adults were dead, as were three babies. Two baby owlets remained, barely hanging on to life. A new neighbor, not knowing about the family of owls, had placed rat poison around their home. The parent owls had scavenged the dead mice and fed them to the babies.

Many rodenticides contain anticoagulants, or blood thinners. The animals succumb to internal bleeding. The owlets were given vitamin K injections, the antidote to this type of rat poison. One baby died, the other recovered and thrived.

Knowing that Godzilla was a female and had almost become a mother, I introduced her to the single baby owlet. She attacked me viciously and grabbed the baby, huddling over it to protect it from this "human enemy." The two owls immediately bonded.

As the baby owlet grew, we moved the pair to an outdoor enclosure. A ramp was built from the floor to the nest box, allowing Godzilla freedom to walk about the cage; the baby owl, now dubbed "Godzilla's Son," began to fly. Under his foster mother's tutelage, the younger owl avoided people but did not have the overt hostility of Godzilla.

One evening as I entered the flight, I was attacked from above. One of the owls had swooped down at my head and flew back up to the nest box. Both owls sat looking down at me, and Godzilla let out a high-pitched scream. Suddenly, she spread her wings and flew across the flight cage for a second strike. I quickly ducked and smiled with excitement—*Godzilla was flying!*

I called Steven Hower, the conservation officer who had originally delivered Godzilla to us, and told him the wonderful story. We discussed
continues on next page

Helping Each Other　*continued from previous page*

releasing the owls back at the poultry farm where Godzilla was found. He would make arrangements at the farm as I prepared the owls for release.

Caring for the owls became tricky now that Godzilla was flying, as entering the cage would be met with a bomber attack. The two owls' feeding time was changed to the morning when the pair was sleeping, and staff would quietly and quickly tidy up while the owls slumbered. Even so, a caregiver needed to wear a leather jacket, gloves, and a motorcycle helmet complete with face shield for protection. It was uncomfortable and comical at the same time, but well worth the trouble when the release day arrived.

Scott Bills, land manager for the game commission, built a nest box for the owls. Hanging the box thirty feet up on the barn, however, required some planning. Steve Hower was driving through Williamstown when he saw a telephone company bucket truck and had an idea.

On the day of the release, I arrived at the farm with one volunteer and two very angry owls. Two bucket trucks were positioned near the

SAFETY

I mentioned earlier that there are risks to your health and safety when rescuing wildlife. This warning should not be taken lightly. Protecting yourself from bites and scratches is a concern, but handling an animal in a way that protects you from exposure to parasites and disease is just as important.

Different animals attack differently, and the effects can be quite damaging. Most people are aware of the danger of claws and teeth from a mammal, but birds can also be very dangerous.

barn, and a small crowd had gathered. Upon arrival, I learned of the combined efforts that had led up to this moment. Several game commission personnel and the Commonwealth Telephone Company, along with the farmer (Dawn Thorne), had sealed the exhaust fans and hung the box. The only thing left to do was place the owls inside; that task was left to me.

As my volunteer and I climbed into the buckets, I tried to calm my fear of heights. We were lifted three stories, and I carefully placed the owls in the box along with one night's meal to get them started. I feared Godzilla would bolt and attack my face, but both owls scurried to the back of the box and hid from the crowd and the sunshine. It was not a glorious release like watching a hawk fly away toward the horizon—but they were free. They would venture from the box in the quiet of night and stake their claim to the surrounding habitat.

As the buckets were lowered, I looked at the crowd beneath me and pondered the joint efforts of the people, organizations, and businesses that brought us to this moment. They applauded as we descended, and we each felt the camaraderie that comes from working together toward a common goal.

But the true miracle here was the owls. Both had been lost and broken, alone and in despair. Both had their lives turned upside down, but together they thrived. Godzilla had helped her foster son grow naturally, and he had given her a reason to fly. They had helped each other, and with the assistance of a group of people who barely knew each other before that day, they were free.

A heron or loon will strike out with its long, pointed beak, aiming for the hands and face. A single strike to an eye can cause serious, permanent injury to (or the loss of) that eye, and, in theory, a well-placed strike could kill a person.

Although its bite can be very painful, a raptor's primary weapon is its feet. The raptor foot, designed for capturing prey, is equipped with long, sharp talons that can be driven deep into the skin—piercing nerves, tendons, and blood vessels. The foot pressure is extremely strong for the bird's size, and the tendons keep the foot

Common loon

closed—making the foot of even a small raptor, such as a screech-owl or American kestrel, difficult to remove. A red-tailed hawk can deliver up to five hundred pounds of pressure per square inch, and a great horned owl can deliver *up to three times that amount of pressure*!

Geese, although a prey species that are large but seemingly un-equipped for battle, can do great harm. Although their feet are harm-less and their beaks can only cause a deep bruise, their wings are formi-dable weapons. At the wrist joint of the wing is a protruding bone called the *alula*. It is hard and sharp and—with the driving force of the powerful wing behind it—can act as a barbed club hitting a person in the face and head.

Traumatic injury is not the only danger to a person rescuing a wild animal. Zoonotic diseases, parasites, and infection can cause long-term problems ranging from a mild irritation to death.

Rabies is a fatal disease common in many areas. Any warm-blooded animal can contract the virus, and prevention from exposure needs to be the first concern when dealing with mammals. Frequently contracted through a bite or scratch from an affected animal, expo-sure can also occur by getting infected saliva into an open scratch, cut, or sore, or by coming in contact with mucous membranes. For more on rabies, see page 100.

Infections from bites can also cause serious conditions even if the animal does not have an active disease. Many animals carry bacteria in their mouths and on their claws that is benign to them, but highly infectious to people. Localized infection may occur, but systemic infection is also a danger. Many years ago, I had a very painful swelling of numerous lymph nodes that turned out to be a *Pasteurella* infection from a bite I received several weeks before. Although the initial wound had healed, the bacteria found a weak part of my body's systems in which to grow. If left untreated, such an infection can cause damage to the body's organs including permanent heart damage.

Another danger when handling wild animals is exposure to parasites. Although there are many, the most noted example is *Baylisascaris procyonis*, or raccoon roundworm. This parasite doesn't seem to cause much harm in its intended host, the raccoon, but can cause severe medical problems when ingested by the wrong host. When ingested by humans, the parasite leaves the digestive tract and circulates through the body by way of the bloodstream, often getting lodged in the smallest of blood vessels, where it becomes a cyst. Depending on the location, the parasite can cause skin irritations or eye and brain damage in humans. If the blood vessels of the eyes or brain are involved, the parasite can result in blindness and even death. The same happens in other unintended hosts such as dogs and cats.

These are only a few examples of the most common dangers of handling wildlife. As you can see, exposure for even a short time can be costly. If you care for and house an animal for any period of time, the threat is heightened and the danger is spread to other family members as well as to pets.

Now that I have outlined a few of the dangers of handling wild animals and emphasized the importance of safety (and if I haven't scared you completely away from saving that creature in need), it's time to talk about helping injured or orphaned animals.

Rehabilitators must wear special gloves and pay careful attention to a raptor's feet when handling it.

Meet the Wildlife Expert

When teaching wildlife capture classes, I emphasize being properly prepared. Preparation includes having the right attitude as well as the proper equipment—and that equipment includes the clothing a person wears.

One late winter afternoon when the ground was thawing but a covering of snow stubbornly clung to it, we got a call about a bobcat with its foot in a trap at a local strip mine. The workers had no way of containing it, but they offered to watch the animal until we arrived.

As we surveyed the land, we talked with the foreman who explained that the mine was closed and being reclaimed. We were warned that certain areas had fresh pools of bio-solids and had not yet been planted with new saplings.

The bobcat was slowly working its way up a hill in a safe area free of bio-solids. Morrie and I approached from the sides. The cat limped and rolled down the hill, then became entangled in some brush. I ran below the cat as Morrie came in from the top. As I began to slide down the snow-covered hill, I realized I was wearing sneakers, not the boots that would have provided me with a sure foothold on the incline. In my rush to secure the proper equipment, I had forgotton to change my clothes for a field capture. I was not dressed properly, and that mistake both saved and exposed my behind that day.

Suddenly, the cat got free of the entanglement and tumbled across the embankment, half trotting and half limping up the hillside. I ran down the bank and over the snow-covered terrain, then suddenly sank into the ground. I landed right in a pool of sludge with one leg buried up to my knee, the other up to my hip. Unaware of my predicament and following the cat's tracks in the snow, Morrie and the mine employees had disappeared over the hilltop. I was on my own.

Trying not to sink in farther, I looked around me. There was nothing I could grab to pull myself out, and every move I made had me sinking deeper. I tried turning, lost my balance, and began to fall backward, which had the benefit of freeing my right leg. My left leg, however, being embedded so firmly in the mire, did not budge. I had not performed a gymnast's "split" in many years and, trying to keep from panicking, made a mental note to do more stretching exercises.

With my right leg now free, I began to press through the sludge to find any firm area that would support me. Finally I hit a solid spot. Shifting my weight, and with all the strength I could muster, I tried to release the suction on my left leg. It was useless; I was trapped.

Suddenly, I remembered my sneakers. Since I wasn't wearing my usual boots, perhaps I could release my shoe. Flexing my foot, I slipped out of my sneaker. The suction released so suddenly, I now found myself chest down in the mire. Ever so slowly, I crept along the top of the biosolids to firm ground minus one sneaker, which was still under the sludge.

As I was walking along the dirt road—in socks, in the snow—I finally got the attention of the mine employees, who came and picked me up. Luckily, the bobcat had freed its foot of the trap while in the entanglement and was now up on a hilltop looking down at us. It was limping slightly but started to run. I knew it would be fine.

I drove home in my sludge-covered clothing that smelled like raw sewage (give me a skunk any day) in bare feet, sitting on a wildlife blanket. I don't know what was in that sludge but I was becoming nauseated.

"New wildlife capture rule number one," I exclaimed, "bring a change of pants."

Before reaching home, we received another emergency call. A redtailed hawk had flown into a rabbit pen and killed a domestic rabbit. The caller was irate and insisted we remove the hawk before it ate any more pet rabbits, "or else!" We first headed home so I could shower and change.

The rabbit pen was a ramshackle shed set against a hillside. Three-quarters of the shed was surrounded by a five-foot fence of chicken wire creating an open-top "yard." The hawk had flown into the fenced area,

continues on next page

Meet the Wildlife Expert *continued from previous page*

eaten its fill of rabbit, and then become entangled in the fence trying to get back out. The bird was bloody and wet and had all but given up.

There was a door in the shed that allowed a person access to the inside, but no gate or doorway led into the fenced area. Small holes were cut in the walls of the shed to allow the rabbits freedom to the fenced area. Since this setup did not allow a person entrance to the yard, I would have to climb over the five-foot fence to reach the hawk. I found the highest ground and began crawling over the fence, when suddenly, the fence caved in.

I successfully got hold of the bird, but now my feet (complete with boots) weren't touching the ground and I couldn't get up. Here I was balanced over a half-collapsed fence, still holding the hawk, and I was about to fall in head first. Morrie and the rabbits' owner grabbed the back of my jeans and pulled me out.

RRRRIIIIPPPP!!

In the car, bird safely in the back, Morrie smirked, "New wildlife capture rule number two—wear a belt!"

THE ANIMAL'S POINT OF VIEW

It doesn't matter how much you love animals or how noble your intentions are; in the animal's mind, you are the enemy. We often encounter people who see an animal suddenly calm down once captured and think "It knows I'm trying to help it." That notion may be romantic, but it is rarely accurate.

Most animals recognize predators instinctively by their eyes. Whereas most prey species have eyes on the sides of their head giving them extended peripheral vision, predators' eyes are on the front of their faces, giving them good depth perception. To an animal, you have the eyes of a predator. If you eat meat, you smell like a predator. If you smile caringly at the animal, you are baring your teeth. From the animal's perspective, they have just lost the life-and-death struggle of predator and prey and are about to become your lunch.

Now add to this the fact that the animal is incapacitated. Wildlife that is sick, injured, or orphaned is already experiencing a great deal of stress. It may be suffering from dehydration, starvation, blood loss, and injury. It will probably be in moderate to severe pain. It will definitely be fearful. The animal doesn't want to be rescued. If given the chance, it would hide in a quiet place and recover or die on its own.

I'm not telling you these things to dissuade you from helping that wild animal but so you will understand the need for minimal handling. The steps you take to help this animal need to include the least amount of handling and movement to reduce the amount of stress to the animal and minimize the danger to you.

DOES THIS ANIMAL TRULY NEED HELP?

Because rescuing an animal does involve danger to you and the animal, your very first question should be "Does this animal really need help?"

With adult animals, it is relatively easy to determine whether or not the animal needs help. Our rule of thumb is "If you can catch it, it's in trouble!"

Juvenile and baby animals are another matter. If there is no obvious injury, perhaps the animal only needs to be left alone or moved to a safe location until its mother returns to retrieve it.

If you are unsure about an animal's need for rescue, the dichotomous keys beginning on page 1 will help you determine the proper steps to take.

Chapter 3

TRUE EMERGENCIES

ADULT ANIMALS

The following signs are considered true emergencies for adult animals:

> Bleeding
> Unconsciousness
> Abnormal use or position of limb(s)
> Odd head position
> Maggots
> Was in a dog's or cat's mouth
> Drainage from eyes or nose
> Behaving abnormally
> Cold and lethargic
> Heat exhaustion and exposure
> Inability to escape

Bleeding is an immediate, life-threatening condition. If possible, every effort should be made to stop the bleeding at the scene. See the "Alleviate Life-threatening Conditions" section for "Bleeding" on page 94.

Unconsciousness is an obvious emergency needing immediate medical attention. Always use caution, however, when handling an unconscious animal. It can recover quite suddenly, and some animals, such as opossums and screech-owls, will feign death when threatened or stressed. Remember, even a seemingly incapacitated animal can be potentially dangerous.

Abnormal use or position of limb(s) may indicate a fracture. Paralysis can be a sign of trauma or illness. Reduce the risk of further injury by placing padding or shredded newspaper in the container and packing the animal tightly enough to impede movement.

Odd head position can be the sign of a head or spinal trauma or disease.

Maggots and fly eggs may or may not accompany an open wound. Maggot eggs on fur or feathers look like cream or yellowish, fuzzy dandruff. This is a sure sign that the animal is in serious trouble. If left untreated, maggots will burrow into wet tissue or openings in the skin and literally eat the animal alive.

If the animal was attacked or carried by a pet, it will need a regimen of antibiotics to prevent infection. Dogs, and especially cats, carry in their mouths bacteria that are highly infectious to wild animals, particularly birds and rabbits.

Drainage from eyes or nose is an indication of illness that needs medical attention. Even if the illness is not contagious or immediately life-threatening, it will impede an animal's ability to hunt or escape predation.

Animals behaving abnormally need to be handled with extreme caution. Rabid animals will often act friendly, as will animals imprinted on humans. Both situations present a great risk to you and anyone assisting you. See the sections on "Rabies" (page 100) and "Imprinting" (page 104).

Cold and lethargic animals are suffering from hypothermia. They are usually in shock and, if not treated immediately, may die suddenly. See the section on "Hypothermia" (page 94).

Heat exhaustion and exposure is another condition requiring immediate attention. See the section on "Hyperthermia" (page 95).

Inability to escape is usually the first sign that an animal is in trouble. Any healthy *adult* animal will not allow itself to be captured or handled.

ENTRAPMENT

Animals often become trapped in our man-made structures such as buildings, window wells, sewage drains, and fences.

Careful examination from a distance should determine whether or not the animal has suffered due to its confinement and is therefore

The Immigrant Owl

I occasionally receive prank calls about purple deer and elephants in people's swimming pools. Often these calls turn out to be a friend or colleague who is teasing and trying to lighten my day. We laugh together and then get down to business. I thought this was one such phone call:

Peggy: "Hello, Red Creek. May I help you?"
Caller: "Hi, this is the garden center and we have a small owl in one of our trees."

Since it was late November, I knew this could not be a baby owl. I assumed it was a smaller species of owl such as the eastern screech-owl or saw-whet owl.

Peggy: "Okay. Is it injured?"
Caller: "It doesn't appear to be. Can you come get it please?"
Peggy: "Ahhh, owls live in trees. What's the problem?"
Caller: "The tree is wrapped in mesh, and the owl is sitting inside."
Peggy: "Can you just unwrap the tree and let it out?"
Caller: "But the tree is inside the building."
Peggy: "Can't you take the tree outside and unwrap it?"
Caller: "You don't understand, I think the owl has been in there several weeks."
Peggy: "A small owl would have starved in that time. It must have gotten in there recently."
Caller: "There are also a lot of bright orange caterpillars on the tree. I think he's been eating them."

Now I believe this to be a joke, but I decide to play along.

Peggy: "Still, you could unwrap the tree and let him go."
Caller: "You don't understand. The tree was delivered here for sale on a truck."
Peggy: "From where?"
Caller: "Florida."
Peggy: "I'll be right over."

I arrived at the garden center, and the scene was exactly as the caller had described: an ornamental tree was tightly wrapped in a fine mesh, and inside the mesh were hundreds of tiny, bright orange caterpillars and one very sorry-looking burrowing owl. We carefully cut the mesh until I could slip my hand inside, and I removed the feathered prisoner.

The owl was emaciated, dehydrated, and had slight feather damage from rubbing against the mesh, but otherwise it seemed unharmed. I called the U.S. Fish and Wildlife Service and reported possession of our immigrant bird.

The bird was a big hit with our volunteers, who, along with me, had never seen this species of owl. Indigenous to the southern states, this owl was not one a Pennsylvania wildlife rehabilitator expected to see. True to the nature of rehabilitators, each volunteer came not only to see the bird but also the bird's bright orange excrement. During the first three days, the cage was splashed with stool so brilliant I expected it to glow—a testament to the presence of the caterpillars.

Within a few days, the owl was flying and gaining weight. It would be ready to be released within a few weeks, but this bird was much too far from home. What to do?

continues on next page

> ## The Immigrant Owl *continued from previous page*
>
> The solution came when a volunteer called to report off for vacation. Her family was driving to Florida for the Christmas holiday. I asked if she could take the owl with her. Along with a cooler of mice, we sent the bird on its way. Her travels found her crossing the Florida border just as the sun was setting in the west—and she set the owl free.
>
> Today, transporting a wayward animal would not be a problem, and I would do things differently. I now network with wildlife rehabilitators around the country and, along with the obligatory permits and reports, a few phone calls would have easily put a relay arrangement together that would have placed that owl back in its natural habitat. But this bird arrived very early in my rehab career; I had not yet made connections with out-of-state wildlife rehabilitators and had not yet learned how easy it is working with wildlife agencies. As a young rehabilitator, new to the idealism that every animal deserves its freedom, I just wanted to get this immigrant owl back home.

in need of extended care. If an animal is trapped but otherwise uninjured, it may need some assistance to help it escape.

It is often not necessary to physically remove an adult animal; it only needs to be given an avenue of escape and a little "quiet time" to feel safe enough to leave.

Birds Trapped in Buildings

The most common situation involving entrapment is a hawk in a large building (such as a commercial structure), but any bird can get inside any building. The bird should first be encouraged to fly out just by opening all the doors and windows, allowing the bird time to leave on its own.

If the bird refuses to leave, or if it is up high and the doors are set much lower than the ceiling, it may need to be shown the route of exit. The trick is to use lighting. Daytime birds usually will not move in the dark. If they cannot see, they will not fly.

Open the largest doors, allowing light to come in, and turn out all the lights in the area. If there are windows that cannot be opened, cover these with cloth or cardboard to cut the light to a minimum. You may need to encourage the bird to leave the safety of its high perch by chasing it until it flies out. Loud noises and soft objects (such as wet sponges) thrown toward the bird will usually get it started.

If there are no doors or windows near the bird, or if the rescue is attempted at night, using the lights-out approach can also work. For this you need several people working together. One person stands by the power to all lighting while the others get ready for the capture. The bird is encouraged to move and, once in flight, the lights are turned off. Unable to see, the bird should land on the floor where a blanket or box can be placed over the bird.

If the bird cannot be easily removed by this procedure, or if it has been trapped for several days, call a local rehabilitator to assist with this bird's return to health and freedom.

Bats in Buildings

Bats can enter a home by accidentally flying through an open door, window, or chimney, or by working their way down from the attic.

A flying bat can be encouraged to leave at night by turning off all the indoor lights and shining a bright light into the doorway from outside. Headlights from a car work very well.

If the bat is clinging to a beam or a curtain, a cup can be placed over the bat and a piece of cardboard slipped under the cup, trapping the bat inside. Release the bat from the cup at the base of a tree, allowing it to crawl up into the tree and roost.

Do not touch the bat. If you are bitten, do not release the bat. It may need to be tested for rabies to ensure your health. If you are bitten, wake up with a bat in your bedroom, or if a bat was in a room with an unattended child, *please* read the section about rabies (page 100) and contact your local department of health immediately.

If bats are getting into your home on a regular basis, you may wish to contact an urban wildlife pest control expert to provide bat exclusion for the building. Removing bats can be done humanely with one-way door systems that allow the bats to leave but do not allow reentry. Once excluded, the entry points are sealed to keep any bats from returning.

Animal has Fallen into a Pit

Most animals will climb out of window wells and other holes if a blanket is secured from top to bottom. The best blankets to use for mammals are loosely woven so they can get their claws into the fabric. Even skunks, the most common animal we see in this predicament, can climb as long as they can dig in their claws. Make sure the blanket is secured well enough to bear the animal's weight.

Leave the animal alone and keep children and pets away. It may take some time for the animal to feel safe enough to leave, and a nocturnal animal may wait until nighttime to make its escape.

BABY ANIMALS: WHAT IS NORMAL AND WHAT IS NOT

A Fallacy that Kills

There is an old wives' tale we frequently hear that is a major factor in baby animals being kidnapped: "If you touch a baby animal, the mother will reject or kill it." This is not true. Mothers *will not* reject their babies because they were touched.

Babies can be safely returned to nests and dens with little risk of rejection. Every precaution should be taken, however, to avoid putting human scent on the babies or at the nest site so the nest is not detected by predators.

Baby Birds and Bird Nests

One of the most common wildlife emergencies we see is baby birds that have fallen out of the nest or the nest itself has fallen. This is an emergency requiring immediate attention that often can be remedied quickly. Babies can be returned to nests, and entire nests can be repaired or replaced completely with great success and little disruption of the family.

If the baby is not injured and has not suffered extreme exposure from heat or cold, every attempt must be made to reunite the baby bird with its parents. No one can raise a baby bird like mom! The

Killdeer

We often hear tales about mother birds pretending to be injured in an effort to lure predators away from the nest. Many birds exhibit this behavior, but the killdeer is the most notable.

Killdeer do not build nests, choosing instead to lay their eggs on a flat gravel area. Stone driveways are a favored spot for killdeer nests because the spotted eggs blend in perfectly with the gravel.

Usually, the first sign of a killdeer nest is not the eggs or a picturesque scene with the mother nestled on the eggs but the pitiful sight of a wounded bird barely able to stand on the lawn. These brown birds with horizontal black-and-white stripes across the face and neck can put on a show that breaks the hardest of hearts.

Killdeer are nature's actresses, and convincing performers they are! Attempting to draw attention away from the eggs, they put on a magnificent display, often limping and dragging a wing. An attempt to capture the bird always ends with its miraculous recovery, and the injured bird flies away.

If a killdeer is found "displaying" near your home, carefully inspect the driveway for eggs. If eggs are found, temporarily block off the area so cars do not drive over the nest. The eggs hatch in about twenty-five days. Once hatched, the precocial babies can immediately follow the mother, and the nest is abandoned.

Killdeer are exceptional birds in that a parent will raise any baby killdeer. If you find a baby killdeer alone or orphaned, it can be placed near a wild mother, who will then adopt it.

baby bird's chances at living a healthy, normal life are greatly increased by allowing nature to raise its own.

If a baby bird has fallen and the nest location is known (and can be reached), simply plop the baby back in the nest and walk away. Check back every few hours to make sure the bird remains in the nest. If it repeatedly falls, check the nest to see if it needs adjustment. A tilted nest will not hold babies well and can be straightened or secured.

Babies being repeatedly thrown from the nest by the parents may have a defect of which the parents are aware. They may not be willing to expend the energy to raise a baby that cannot survive. Such a bird can be taken to a wildlife rehabilitator.

Occasionally, sibling rivalry will cause a weaker baby to be thrown. In some cases, a parasitic bird species may be the culprit. Cowbirds, when hatched in a host nest, will push all the other birds out of the nest. This is nature at its finest but may be difficult to witness in your own backyard. In this case, consult your local rehabilitator for advice. They may take and raise the babies who have been victimized.

If an entire nest has fallen, the nest can be placed in a wicker basket or kitchen colander and hung in the same tree. The container doesn't matter as long as it's unobtrusive and has excellent drainage. Locating the nest near the original spot increases the probability of success but isn't essential. Often the parents will continue to feed even if the nest is hung in a nearby tree, which may be necessary if the nest accident occurred because a tree fell or was removed. Parent birds are usually very accepting of the nest being disturbed for a short period of time.

The following are examples of nests being moved entirely that were very successful.

In one case, the nest was removed from a cavity in a building because new siding was being placed on the house. After the siding was installed, we wired a five-gallon bucket on its side under the drain spouting and slid the nest and babies inside. The mother only took a few minutes to return and start feeding the hungry babies.

The second move was an intricately planned project that took some ingenuity. A family owned a farm tractor and needed to put it in service. As they were clearing the brush around it, they saw a robin fly out. Looking closer, they found a nest built under the tractor body containing four blue eggs.

We were called for advice. They wanted to move the tractor and needed it for their livelihood but did say they could wait one to two weeks, but no longer than that. There was no chance that the babies

would hatch and fledge in that time. There was little chance of a mother robin staying on eggs if the nest had been moved. Also, there was not a nearby location where the nest could be placed.

Because it is the sound of the babies' feeding calls that attracts the parents, waiting for the babies to hatch increased our chances for a successful move of the nest.

During that time, we prepared a new nest site by moving a table next to the tractor, at the same height. The table was situated as close to the nest as possible, and beneath it we hung an empty wicker basket. This gave the mother time to adjust to the presence of the table. The babies began hatching four days later.

After a few days, when we heard the first babies calling strongly, we moved the entire nest with the babies to the basket beneath the table. The parents began feeding almost immediately. After two more days the tractor was removed. The farmer resumed his work, as did the robin parents.

That hatch not only thrived and fledged a few weeks later, but the parents chose the same location beneath the table for a second clutch of babies later that season!

Baby Rabbits

Cottontail nests are often found by children and pets. Others are discovered after an accident such as happens when mowing the lawn. Calls often come from people simply worried that they have not seen the mother since discovering the nest, fearing she has abandoned it. A mother rabbit, however, will not reject her young if the nest was disturbed or the babies were touched.

Baby rabbits have no body odor because their scent glands do not develop until they begin to mature. This protects the nest from predators that hunt by smell. The mother doesn't want to place her odor at the nest, so she only feeds two or three times during the night and only for short periods. She is often never seen.

Cottontail rabbits are independent and able to care for themselves at about five inches long. They are fully weaned, eating vegetation, and the mother is no longer caring for them. They may or may not still be "hanging out" with siblings at the nest. It's not unusual to find one sitting still in an area, and it may not try to escape upon approach.

Because they cannot yet run fast, they often will remain still and attempt to use camouflage to avoid predators. Aside from visual camouflage, at this age they still do not put off an odor. Their fur absorbs smells around them—a type of "odor camouflage." If the bunny remains completely still, a predator may walk right by—never knowing the animal was there. Because of this, you can easily walk up to a young rabbit and pick it up. It will then squirm trying to escape the predator's (your) grasp.

If the location found is unsuitable or dangerous because of people and pets, the rabbit can be relocated.

Signs of a Problem

Flies around the nest are an indication that there are one or more dead babies or the presence of blood in the nest. A mower accident will often wound or kill one or two babies, while the others are untouched. The blood from the injured bunnies will attract flies, and the nest should be rescued.

A "sunken" appearance on both sides of the spine is an indication that the rabbit is dehydrated and starving. Any rabbit that was in a dog's or cat's mouth should be treated with antibiotics.

Let Me Check My Wallet

Baby rabbits are still quite small when they become independent. Being able to determine their age and size over the phone can save the caller the time and trouble of rescuing an animal that doesn't need help. Often a person can release the rabbit into a nearby area, avoiding an unnecessary trip to our center. Trying to communicate the size of a small animal, however, can be frustrating.

If simply asked "how big is the rabbit?" we often hear "it fits in the palm of my hand." Well, both a golf ball and a baseball can fit that description. I've also discovered that people have difficulty determining length. I've received rabbits reported to be four inches long that were actually twice that size and quite independent.

One day I came up with what I thought was the perfect solution: A dollar bill is six inches long. If a bunny is three-quarters that size or larger, it can take care of itself. I was immensely proud of myself, and my newfound communication tool helped many rabbits avoid an unnecessary "taxi ride" to our facility.

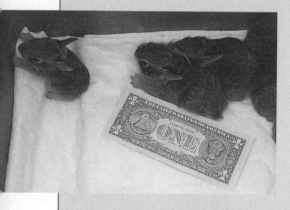

One day I received a call about a small bunny that had fallen into a window well. It appeared uninjured, but the caller wanted to be sure it was old enough to be on its own before releasing it. I recited my perfect question: "A dollar bill is six inches long. Is your bunny half that size? Three quarters? Or is it longer than a dollar bill?"

I was asked to "hold on," and I waited as I pictured the woman taking a dollar from her wallet. The wait became extended until finally the distraught woman returned. She had a terrible dilemma: She did not have a single. She only had a five-dollar bill, so she could not tell me the size of the creature.

Repairing Rabbit Nests

This procedure is best done before nightfall.

Return any surrounding fur to the nest depression.

Place the babies in the nest, and cover loosely with natural grasses and dirt from the nest area.

Lay a piece of yarn or string loosely over the nest in an X shape before evening. Do not check again until morning. Check the nest the next morning to see if the yarn has been moved. If it has been moved, mom was back and all is well.

If the yarn is the same as you left it the night before, the reintroduction failed. Remove the babies from the nest and take them to a rehabilitator.

Relocating Rabbits

Rabbits can be relocated at five inches long or larger.

Resist the temptation to hold, carry, stare at, or talk to the rabbit. This rabbit recognizes predators by their eyes (predators' eyes are on the front of their head—not on the side like the mother's eyes are). If it calms down when you look at it or talk to it, it doesn't realize you are friendly. It thinks you are about to eat it and is becoming stressed, preparing to die. If you need to take it any distance, put it in a closed box for transportation.

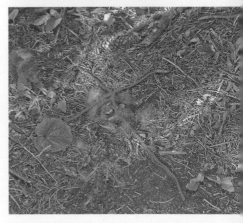

A dollar bill, which is six inches long, can be used to determine the rabbit's size.

Take the rabbit to a nearby area where there are pine trees near natural grasses or lawn that is not treated for insects or weeds. Dandelion and clover are favorite "first foods." Choosing a location with these weeds is optimal.

It is a fallacy that you will harm an animal by touching it. Preserving its odor camouflage is important, however, so place the bunny under a pine tree. Pines are strong-smelling, will hide the baby, and will also protect it from sun and rain.

Fawns

People often find fawns and think that they have been orphaned or abandoned. The fawn will be seen day after day, in the exact same place—alone. They are cute, appear fragile, and are hard to resist. It can be difficult to just walk away.

Like the cottontail's, a fawn's scent glands develop as it matures, so a young fawn will have no body odor. This protects it from predators. The mother doesn't want to place her odor in the area so she only visits for short periods, often during the night. Her presence endangers the baby, so she must leave it alone.

Unless a fawn is injured or obviously weak and lethargic, leave it alone.

Fawns found in a dangerous location, such as on or near a roadway, can be moved one to two hundred yards away. Place the fawn in high grass, a nearby thicket, or a forest and walk away. If the fawn follows you, put it back, scold it, and make it stay. The mother will find it when the area is quiet and she feels safe.

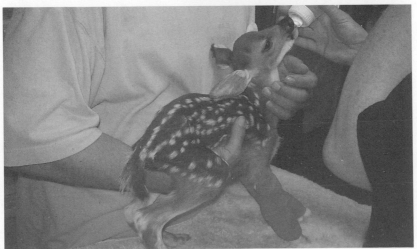

Only an experienced rehabilitator can provide an injured fawn the help it needs.

A Fawn in Trouble

You, the reader, may get tired of listening to me proclaim "Take that wild animal to a rehabilitator! Follow their instructions!" Too often, however, I am handed another perfect example of why I am so stern about these instructions.

An extremely healthy fawn had been orphaned only hours earlier when its mother was hit by a car. After giving the caller directions to our center and instructions on containing the baby deer, we waited . . . and waited . . . and waited. No fawn arrived, and the telephone number we had been given was not genuine. We had no way of following up on the situation.

Four days later, a man called asking me to take the *now-injured* fawn. I gave strict instructions on how to contain the fawn (box it up) for the ride, yet the fawn arrived wrapped in a blanket, on the man's lap in the back of a Ford Explorer.

There was blood everywhere—on the deer, the blanket, and the man—and was sprayed throughout the back of the vehicle. As I took note of a three-inch gash on the man's arm, I realized that the blood wasn't all from the deer. Deer have very sharp hooves.

The fawn was quite friendly and had suffered dehydration resulting from diarrhea. We were told that the young buck had been living in the man's home, had been fed cow's milk, and was allowed to sleep in bed. He had also been allowed to make friends with the family's German shepherd because, the man believed, herding breeds would never attack a herd animal.

The fawn's immediate injury was obvious as blood ran freely from his tongue, which was protruding from the side of his mouth. The fawn had approached the dog while the dog was eating and, according to the man, the shepherd just "snapped at its face." The fawn almost lost half of his tongue, which was split sideways.

When asked why the man kept the deer and didn't follow through with my advice four days prior, I was told "it was such a wonderful experience for the family."

"A mighty high price the fawn paid for your enjoyable experience. The cost may be the fawn's life!" I told them.

Looking at the tongue, I thought the young buck would probably lose it completely. Would the deer be able to eat, drink, and swallow without a tongue? I didn't know. I called our veterinarian, Dr. Bridget McMahon, and my hopes fell as I was told she was away on vacation.

We were trying to locate another large animal vet when Dr. McMahon called back. She was driving in from her vacation to help.

We met her at her practice, Kutztown Animal Hospital, and the deer was rushed into surgery. Fortunately, the blood supply to the torn flesh was not interrupted, and the fawn would not lose his tongue. When the suturing was done, he had a perfectly shaped—albeit very swollen— tongue. I was thrilled.

Our elation was crushed during recovery when the fawn did not want to wake up. Losing their ability to flee, prey species often have complications with anesthesia and will just shut down. An hour later, we left with a bundled baby deer sleeping in the back of the van.

continues on next page

A Fawn in Trouble *continued from previous page*

Once back at the center, I checked on him every fifteen minutes. I'd see an ear twitch or an eye twitch, but nothing else. Attempts to stir him yielded nothing, and late that evening we went to bed.

During the night I woke to a beautiful sound—the mournful cries of a very hungry fawn. He was on his feet and demanding to be fed. The vet had warned that, because of the tongue's swelling and loss of mobility, I would probably have to intubate him for a week or more, but I tried a bottle anyway. The deer sucked down a full eight ounces of sucrose. *Sucked!* By the next morning, he looked completely normal and could easily drink from a bottle.

This story has a happy ending. My veterinarian did fabulous work, and the fawn quickly regained his health. A few days later, he was introduced to other fawns so he would learn to be the wild animal he was born to be.

The deer was released nearby a few months later and can occasionally be seen grazing the hill behind the wildlife center. Thankfully, he never approaches, and anyone who isn't familiar with his story would never know that this magnificent buck once slept in a bed and made friends with a German shepherd.

Signs of a Problem

> Obvious injury or weak and lethargic
> Fawn is found with the dead mother
> Flies humming around the fawn
> Maggots or fly eggs on the fur
> A sunken appearance
> Spiky, fluffy-looking fur
> Laying flat on its side unable to stand
> Walking around and loudly crying for hours

Opossums

It's normal for most animal babies to be found for periods of time without mom, but opossums are one of the few babies that are *never* left alone. They cannot survive on their own.

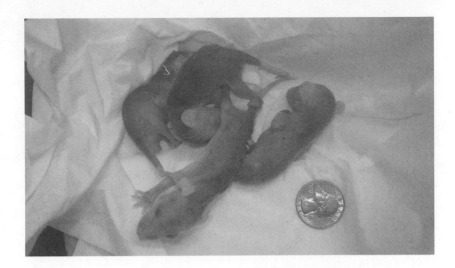

When they are born, opossums are embryonic and only the size of a pencil's eraser. They crawl into the mother's pouch and remain there for about two months. After leaving the pouch, they hitch a ride on mother's back, staying with her until they are six or more inches long without the tail.

Mother opossums are often killed on the road, but the babies remain alive, sometimes uninjured in the pouch or scattered about on the roadway. Check the pouch in mom's abdomen for remaining babies. She can have up to thirteen. Sometimes the baby simply falls off the mother, and she may keep going, unknowingly abandoning it.

These are true emergencies, for without its mother, a baby opossum will die.

When hungry, an opossum will make a repeated sneezing sound. It does not have a cold—it is hungry.

This rehabilitator releases opossums old enough to care for themselves.

One by One

The amount of trouble a person will go to when helping an animal is often heartwarming. I received a call one stormy night asking only for directions to our center. The gentleman on the phone said he found a

mother opossum killed on the road and had rescued the babies. We awaited his arrival and prepared the incubator for our newest patients.

A short time later, a large handicapped-equipped van pulled up our driveway. The rain was pouring down, and we noticed the driver was struggling to exit the vehicle. Morrie and I went out to assist, and we met a most selfless man whose personal struggles did not stop him from helping ten little creatures in need.

We often receive calls from people who want to do no more than report an injured animal. These people often tell us they have no time, courage, or desire to personally intervene. A post-polio victim, the man standing before us with the aid of forearm crutches and leg braces had

Catching Baby Opossums

If a mother opossum has been killed and the babies have scattered into the surrounding area, you may have to trap the babies.

Take a five-gallon bucket (for small opossums) or a garbage can (for larger ones) and place it against a fence, tree, or other easy-to-climb surface. Place a strong-smelling, opened can of cat food inside the container. The opossums will be able to climb up and jump into the container but will not be able to climb back out.

Leave the container out all night and you should catch all of the babies in the area.

every reason to not stop and help. It was nighttime, raining, and moving about under the best conditions took great effort for him.

We asked this gentle soul how he had managed to rescue the baby opossums. He explained that he had to kneel to grasp each animal, place it in his shirt pocket, and return each to the van, where he wrapped them in a sweatshirt. Since he needed to use both crutches, and only one baby at a time would fit in his pocket securely, he repeated this procedure ten times in the torrential downpour. We offered him a hot coffee and a chance to dry and warm himself. He declined, saying he had to be on his way.

As we watched him struggle to enter the van, which was equipped with hand controls, we realized the amount of labor it took for him to retrieve these fortunate babies, one by one. Although his body was handicapped, his spirit was not, and ten opossums had a chance to grow and be released back to a life of freedom.

Squirrels

Squirrel nests are often destroyed when a tree is cut down. This may or may not be an emergency. Given the opportunity, the mother will sometimes retrieve an uninjured baby and carry it to a new location, but she will not approach if people are near.

An uninjured baby squirrel can be placed in a box near the tree and watched for a short time from a distance, preferably through a window from indoors. This may result in the mother rescuing it. Wait a few hours or until dark. Do not leave the babies out past sunset.

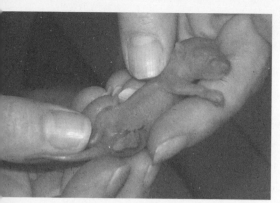

This baby squirrel had to be treated with antibiotics after being attacked by a cat.

Squirrels are one of the only baby animals that typically will "ask for help" when in trouble. A hungry, baby squirrel may approach you, often climbing onto your shoes or up your pant leg.

How can you tell if a young squirrel is old enough to be on its own? Look at the hairs on the tail. If they stand upright, fanning out completely perpendicular to the tail, it is weaned.

Signs of a Problem

Injury such as broken limbs

Bleeding, bruising, and "crustiness" around the nostrils (a sign of a concussion needing medical treatment)

Screaming babies on the ground or clinging to trees

Maggots or fly eggs on the fur or in the ears

Young squirrels may need the help of a rehabilitator if the mother can't be found.

Box turtle with a broken shell

Turtles

Wildlife rehabilitators have made great progress in saving injured and sick turtles. New methods of shell repair have been very successful, and the turtles respond well to antibiotic therapy as well as to treatment for parasites.

Healthy animals that are in a dangerous area such as on a highway can be moved a short walking distance to a safer location. Make sure to relocate the turtle in the same direction it was headed, or it may retrace its steps back to where you picked it up.

Examine turtles for bleeding, cracked shells, and maggots. Examine the nostrils, eyes, and ears for any discharge or swelling. Any of these signs are life-threatening for the turtle.

Do not handle turtles more than absolutely necessary. Turtles carry bacteria that can make a person sick. *Your* bacteria can also make *them* sick, causing respiratory, eye, and ear infections.

Wash your hands with an antibacterial soap before eating, drinking, or smoking.

Painted turtle with an ear abscess

A Note on the Eastern Box Turtle

The eastern box turtle population has dropped considerably over the past few decades. Research has found that box turtles may not have the ability to lure a mate through vocalizations, scents, or behavior. Breeding relies solely on turtles seeing each other. Since mating is made possible only by one turtle accidentally meeting another, population density is very important. The sparser the population, the less chance there is for an accidental meeting, and the less chance of a successful breeding. The situation spirals downward from there.

Eastern box turtle with an eye infection

It is also believed that adult box turtles do not survive long outside their normal, personal range. Evidence suggests that a box turtle that is moved too great a distance will not hibernate the next winter. One of the factors contributing to the decline of the eastern box turtle may be well-meaning people moving turtles to a "better" location for the turtle's safety.

When rescuing a box turtle, it is extremely important that you document exactly where it was found so it can be returned to the exact area, where it may hibernate through the winter.

Chapter 4

CAPTURE

*I*f you have a situation in front of you and are looking for quick instruc-
tions, please take the time to review the previous chapter. The choices
you make and the actions you take will not only affect the animal you are
rescuing, but can also affect your life and health as well as that of your fam-
ily and pets.

You have a wildlife situation. You are aware of the dangers to you
and the stress that capture will place on the animal. You have also
determined the animal is in need of help. So how does one safely capture a wild animal?

Each species is different, and each situation has its own problems.
Some animals are easily captured with nets and blankets while others
require the use of gloves. It takes experience to perfect these techniques, and even with experience and expertise you can be injured.
No book or written instructions can teach all these methods safely,
but we do have one way that works for most situations.

THE BOX-OVER METHOD

The best way to protect yourself is to never touch the animal in the
first place. When giving directions for wildlife capture, my preferred
instruction is the box-over method. With this method you can capture
most animals safely without touching the animal, and the animal
never touches you.

To capture an animal with this method you need an appropriately
sized container such as a cardboard box that is large enough to snugly
fit the animal in. The box needs to be strong enough to keep the
animal from escaping, breaking out, or—for mammals such as

63

woodchucks—chewing through. For large animals that are too strong for a cardboard box, a metal trash can works well.

This capture container will also be your transport device and will therefore need ventilation. Most cardboard boxes breathe without additional ventilation, but if you are planning on using a container that will be airtight, several small holes placed near the top of the container will allow for air exchange.

When capturing the animal, this container will be slipped over the animal, upside down, trapping the animal in the container against the ground.

You also need a stiff, thin piece of cardboard, metal, plastic, or wood that is larger than the opening of the container. You can use the lid of the box if there is one. Once the container is over the animal, this stiff sheet or lid is used to slide under the container between the animal and the ground.

You will also need tape to secure the two pieces together. Duct tape or strong packing tape both work well for this.

Once you have everything you need, approach the animal slowly. If the animal is mobile, you may need several people to cut off its escape routes. Make sure the direction away from you does not have hazards such as traffic, water, or thick briars where the animal may flee and experience further injury.

The box-over method is used to capture small animals, such as this owl, and large ones.

When you are close enough, quickly place the container over the animal, trapping it inside.

Hold the container down firmly for a moment until the animal stops struggling.

Slowly work the thin, stiff board under the edge of the container and slide it between the animal and the ground. You may have to use a gentle sawing motion to get the board completely under, or wiggle the container to push the animal on top of the board. Work slowly until the board is past all the edges of the container.

Once done, you have successfully contained the animal without touching it. You can now secure the lid or stiff sheet to the container with heavy tape. Very carefully roll the container until it is upright and secure the "packaging" some more.

HOW TO CAPTURE A DUCK

Ducks pose unique problems when injured. If they can't fly, they can still run and swim and, even injured, will take to water for protection. Attempts to capture injured waterfowl often result in the proverbial "wild goose chase" and may end in failure. It can be done, however, with the proper planning, techniques, and equipment.

More than one person is usually needed to catch waterfowl. If the bird is on land and can be lured in with food, two people will usually suffice. If the bird is on water or must be chased onto land, many more hands will be needed.

A duck should be held with its wings pressed close to its body.

Hand Capture

Many people think nets are the easiest way to catch ducks, but in my experience even the tamest hand-fed ducks will flee at the sight of a net. Anything out of the ordinary will send them scurrying away from you.

If the duck is accustomed to being hand-fed, you can lure it in with seed or bread. Sit on the ground and try to coax the bird close to you. Patience is the key to gaining its trust. You will only have one chance, so make it a good one. Once the bird knows you are trying to catch it, it will not come near you again.

When the bird is close enough, you can throw a towel or sheet over it. If the bird is nervous, even the strangeness of a cloth will be enough to scare it away. In that case, you may have to grab the bird with your hands.

Don't grab the neck, wings, or legs as this could injure the bird further.

To grab a duck successfully on land, position your hands over the top of its wings and gently push the bird toward the ground. Once you have the bird and wings controlled, have a second person approach and drape a towel or sheet over the bird's head.

Lift the bird gently, holding its wings securely against its body, and place the bird inside a cardboard box that has fold-in flaps. While securely holding the bird in the bottom of the box, have a second person fold in the flaps. Do not let go until the last flap is being folded closed. Hold the flaps in place while the other person secures the box with tape.

Land Capture

A wary duck or goose that is mobile on land will need to be corralled into a trap or safe area for hand capture. Several people will be needed to cut off the bird's escape routes and encourage the bird to flee into your trap.

A careful examination of the area will offer suggestions on which way to chase the bird. You want to avoid chasing the bird into the water or areas that may be dangerous.

An empty garage, barn, or fenced yard can serve as a corral area, as can several people with nets or blankets hiding in a small area. Your chase group would then create a semicircle around the bird with the opening toward the planned capture area.

To extend your semicircle with fewer people, you can cover a larger area by holding blankets between each person, creating a visible wall that the bird believes it cannot pass. One person can create the same effect with two

blankets and two long sticks (such as broom handles) held out to the side as shown on the previous page.

Do not run after the bird. It may take some time and patience to get the bird tired enough so it stops running. You want to tire the bird while conserving your energy so the bird tires before you do.

Water Capture

The trick to capturing a bird that's on the water is to get it to flee to the land where capture can be achieved using the techniques outlined previously. How the bird is persuaded to leave the water will depend on the size of the lake or pond involved.

> **WARNING:**
> **When working near water, beware of soft ground and mud. You could sink and be stranded, thus requiring rescue yourself.**
>
> *Always work in teams when rescuing in a wetlands area.*

If the pond is small enough to cast a fishing line across, chasing the bird from the water can be quite easy.

Have two people stand on either side of the pond. On one side, group 1 has a casting pole for fishing with a heavy weight to cast completely across the pond. On the other side, group 2 has two long pieces of floating rope or plastic carpenter's tape (orange works best), each long enough to reach across the pond.

Group 1 casts the fishing line across the pond to group 2. The end of each rope or tape is loosely tied to the end of the fishing line; group 1 then reels the line back in, bringing the rope ends toward it. After removing the fishing line, each person takes an end of one rope and moves apart, stretching the rope over the pond in an X fashion. Keep each rope taut about eighteen inches above the water.

Working together, you can now approach the duck, encouraging it with the rope to move. If the duck attempts to jump the rope, raise it and slap the rope off the water. If the bird dives under the water, wait for it to surface and start over.

Motorboats can be used to rescue injured waterfowl too far from land.

Many ducks will leave the water right away, but others may continuously avoid the rope by diving under or jumping over it. Again, patience is the key and you will have to tire the duck out until it leaves the water.

For extremely large bodies of water, it will be necessary to use motorboats or remote-controlled toy boats to chase the bird toward the landing you wish it to take. Two or more manned motorboats can string the same type of orange carpenter's tape or floating rope between the boats to encourage the bird to move toward land. Once on land, have a team waiting to begin the land chase toward a trap.

GEESE

With a few modifications, an injured goose can be captured in the same manner as a duck. Because of their size, geese can be dangerous and can injure you if handled incorrectly. They cannot be hand-captured in the same manner as you would a duck.

Geese have a hidden weapon that is quite formidable. This weapon, called the *alula*, is a sharp bone protruding from the wrist area of the wing. With a strong slap of the wing, the alula can cut skin and cause bruises and contusions. A well-directed blow to the head can stun a person or cause a mild concussion.

These birds are best hand-captured by having two people throw and hold a blanket down over the bird. A box can then be worked over the bird; capture is completed by using the box-over method outlined on page 63.

HERONS, EGRETS, AND OTHER FISHING BIRDS

Fishing birds with long pointed beaks are one of the most dangerous birds to handle. They prey on fish and therefore have deadly aim with their beaks. Because many have long necks and legs, they can extend their reach much farther than one would expect. When approaching a fishing bird, it is quite possible that the bird can reach out and injure you before you are even close enough to touch it.

We never work with these types of birds without full eye protection that covers the eyes completely, including the sides. Eyeglasses do not offer enough protection because the slightest mishap can cause severe eye damage and even permanent blindness. This is not a bird with which to take chances, for it may cost you your sight!

Note the eye protection on both handlers.

Wearing both eye protection and gloves, use the box-over method outlined on page 63. Approach the bird from its front, keeping the box between you and the bird. Once close enough, place the box down over the bird to enclose it.

If you cannot effectively capture the bird in this manner, you may need to use a blanket to first render it helpless. You may also need two people for this method, and again, both people must wear eye protection and gloves.

Walk toward the bird with the blanket in front of you and drape it over the bird completely. Once the bird is covered, feel through the

Two people may be needed to capture a large waterbird, such as this great blue heron.

Firmly hold the beak of the heron to prevent injury.

Have a second person lift the heron into a holding container.

Make sure the heron fits comfortably in the container and has enough ventilation.

Do not let go of the beak until the container is almost completely closed.

blanket for the beak. Hold the beak securely as a second person lifts the body of the bird. *Do not let go of that beak!*

Working together, lower the bird and the blanket into the travel container. Place the lid on the container or fold in the flaps of the box while still holding on to the beak. Release the beak as the box is quickly closed and secured.

LOONS AND GREBES

Loons and grebes are also fishing birds with long necks and sharp beaks. The same precautions need to be followed as with herons and egrets.

There is one exception that is significant and, although it aids in easy capture, is the reason they often become incapacitated: loons and grebes can walk on land only with great difficulty.

The legs on a loon-type bird are adapted for swimming and hunting fish underwater (very much like a penguin or seal). The legs are short and set far back and to the sides. The body and chest are quite heavy, making it impossible for the bird to stand up on its legs.

Loons and grebes live exclusively on large bodies of water, leaving only to nest by crawling up on the bank, a sand bar, or a large snag. To

Arctic loon

Even when releasing this loon, the handler made sure to wear eye protection.

fly, they must first gain speed by swimming below the surface, then breaking above the surface, flapping their wings while running on top of the water. The body of water must be large enough to allow the bird to gain enough momentum before reaching land.

In flight, these birds look for large bodies of water on which to land. Occasionally, a wet roadway or parking lot can be mistaken for water, and the bird will crash on the hard surface and become stranded. This often happens in winter where snow- and ice-covered roads are mistaken for partially frozen lakes and rivers. Once on the ground, the bird can neither walk nor fly and, if not rescued, will become injured from resting on the hard surface or will die.

In this case, the bird is usually not injured except for small cuts and scrapes on its feet. Often the bird only needs to be returned to a large, open body of water where it can resume its normal life.

Do not mistake this bird's inability to walk as helplessness. These birds have the same long neck and pointed beak of a heron with just as accurate of an aim. They will immediately strike for the eyes, and anyone attempting a rescue needs to wear full eye protection.

RAPTORS

Raptors offer an additional challenge to capture because they use both their feet and beaks for protection. The beaks are curved and sharp, designed for tearing flesh. A bite from a raptor can inflict a serious wound, yet the feet and talons are the primary weapons. The talons of a great horned owl are about an inch long, and the estimated power of its grip is from 500 to 1,500 pounds per square inch. Even a small raptor such as an American kestrel or screech-owl can inflict an open, painful wound; what the smaller raptors lack in size, they seem to make up for with tenacity.

Because of their foot strength, no attempt for capture should ever be made without gloves and eye protection. All-leather welding gloves will protect your hands from most raptors except the larger birds such as great horned owls.

Although they can fight fiercely, even when injured, raptors must be handled carefully to prevent further injury. Every precaution must

be taken to avoid feather damage through handling, since feathers must be in top condition for the bird to survive once released. The box-over method (described on page 63) is your best choice for capture.

Covering a daytime raptor with a blanket will quiet it quickly. Hawks especially become calm in the dark. This can prevent escape while minimizing further damage, giving you a chance to get a better grip on the bird.

A severely injured raptor, or one that is in shock, may lie face down, allowing you to pick it up. With the bird face down and its head away from you, place your hands about halfway down the back on each side of the bird to control its wings. Slide your fingers down under the bird until you feel its legs, keeping your

Notice the sharp talons on this great horned owl.

Wildlife Detective

Early one October morning, we received a male red-tailed hawk with an unusual problem. Although seemingly quite fat and healthy and with no visible injuries, he could not fly. On closer inspection, we noticed the bird smelled like burnt hair—the feathers on one side of his body, including those on his wing, had been melted!

One of the biggest problems when working with wildlife is that they cannot tell you what happened to them, and, unlike with pet animals, the incident is rarely witnessed. I had wondered why an apparently healthy adult bird would venture close enough to fire or heat to allow it to become burned. Had the bird suffered another injury, such as head trauma, prior to the melting of his feathers? Was he sick?

Discovering the cause was important to the bird's treatment. As wildlife rehabilitators, we often have to "play detective." My first question was about the environment where the bird was found—a small suburban town with blocks of individual homes on small lots. We were told there was one factory that had high, industrial-style smokestacks, but there was not much else in the area. The smokestacks and chimneys of the homes were the only real sources of heat we could find, but we were still left with the question of why this hawk would approach or land on a hot chimney.

That evening, I was pondering this very question when I heard my house furnace turn on. Normally, this would have gone unnoticed, except that it was the first time it had turned on that autumn season. I suddenly had an answer.

Octobers in Pennsylvania are beautiful. Not only are the trees ablaze with autumn's colorful display, the daytime temperatures range around a comfortable seventy degrees. While the daytime hours are warm enough to wear short sleeves, the nighttime temperatures are cool and crisp.

Hawks are active during the day and sleep deeply during the night. I have often entered our hawk flight enclosures during the night and the birds slept on undisturbed. If this hawk had been perched, sleeping on a chimney, he may not have immediately noticed the change in temperature. The bird may have slept through the initial melting of his feathers

until pain forced him away and he fluttered to the ground. A nocturnal owl would have never been caught in such a situation.

I now believed I had a completely healthy bird with feather damage. Blood tests confirmed its healthy state, so the hawk was moved outside into the flight enclosure with other hawks. Although we can repair a few feathers by imping (splinting donor feathers and inserting them into the injured bird's feather shafts), there were too many feathers involved for a procedure such as this. The hawk (who my volunteers named "Smokey") would have to wait until he molted his feathers the following July.

Smokey appeared quite content in the "flight"; he was eating the free food and socializing with the other red-tailed hawks. He did not, however, want anything to do with humans. When volunteers would arrive with that day's menu, he would stay as far away as possible, waiting until they left to take his portion.

By the end of June, he had started growing new feathers. It would soon be time to release him.

continues on next page

Wildlife Detective *continued from previous page*

During his nine-month stay, several hawks had been introduced to the flight, and Smokey had witnessed several more being released. I would enter the flight enclosure fully gloved, grab a bird that was doing well, carry it out of the pen, and then release it to the sky.

At some point, Smokey must have understood what was happening and knew his time had come. It was a hot morning in mid-July. I entered the flight to feed, and Smokey flew up to the perch closest to me and looked me squarely in the eyes. He never flinched as I slowly walked around him, inspecting his feathers. Each burnt feather had been replaced by a perfect, new feather. It was time.

I'd like to be able to say that he allowed me to gently pick him up and carry him to his freedom—but that didn't happen. When I returned with my gloves, he panicked and flew away from me. John, a volunteer on his way to becoming a veterinarian, helped me catch him, and we carried him from the enclosure.

John slowly raised the bird, and he stood upright on his hand. Smokey paused and looked around. Slowly he spread his wings and lifted. Flying strongly over the field below, the hawk alighted high in a tree across a field. His name was no longer Smokey. At that moment he was once again an anonymous, but magnificent, red-tailed hawk that flies over the land. He let out a piercing scream.

Red-tailed hawks are screamers. Many will vocalize loudly after release. I am not sure if it is a scream of joy or simply them announcing their presence in the habitat. On this day, however, I like to think it was a "thank you."

thumbs above to hold the wings. Pull the legs back toward the tail, grasping the body, wings, tail, and legs in one grip. Picking the bird up in this manner also allows you to place the bird feet down and facing away from you in the holding box.

Often the bird will try to flee or fight you. After attempting to flee and failing, or after being cornered, a raptor will turn and face you. It may puff out its feathers, appearing large and fierce, in an attempt to scare you away. It may vocalize, click its beak, or make other gestures to back you down. It will then roll back on its tail, exposing its feet (its primary weapons) toward you.

Remember, no matter how fierce the bird is acting, it is extremely frightened and fighting for its life. The capture method you choose should minimize its fear.

If you cannot use a blanket or box because of the terrain or location, then you will need to grab the bird. One method is to allow the bird to grab your gloved hand, and then you grab its legs from behind, between the fingers of your other hand. Getting one finger between its legs will help keep the bird from twisting. If the bird releases its hold on you, you can then support the chest with your free hand.

This last method does have many drawbacks and should only be used as a last resort. You cannot grab a bird in this manner if there is a chance of a leg or hip injury. Holding a bird this way also does not control its wings, which will flap frantically, probably in your face (another good reason to be wearing your goggles).

Other Capture Suggestions

The box-over method may not be necessary in all capture situations. We offer the following suggestions with the additional warning for you to use common sense and consider your safety first.

- Never put a bird in a wire cage. Wire cages (even bird and parrot cages) will fray and break feathers, which the bird needs to fly perfectly. Damaged feathers will impede its ability to survive and may result in an unnecessarily extended rehabilitation time.

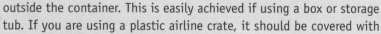

- Choose a container that is large enough to not damage feathers, yet small enough to prevent excessive movement.

- Wild animals will feel more secure if they cannot see outside the container. This is easily achieved if using a box or storage tub. If you are using a plastic airline crate, it should be covered with a blanket to obstruct the animal's view.

- Keep baby animals together to share body heat. One inventive way to transport baby opossums or squirrels is to place them together inside a pillowcase. Tie the pillowcase shut and place it inside the transport box.

- Never lay an unconscious animal on its back. Lay an unconscious bird or mammal face down, slightly to the side.
- Give a bird something to hold on to. Place a baby blanket, sweatshirt, or t-shirt in the bottom of the container for the bird to grasp with its feet. Never place bath towels or bed sheets inside the container with the animal, as these can unravel and create an entanglement.
- Attempt to pad the animal. Fill the container over half full with finely shredded newspaper. This will support the animal on all sides, keeping it from rolling or banging on the inside of the container. Blankets padding the sides of the box will serve the same purpose. Again, make sure the cloth cannot unravel and ensnare the animal.
- When packaging a mammal for transport, use the same considerations you would use for a bird. Make sure the animal cannot see outside the container and that it has proper ventilation. Supply padding such as shredded newspaper or blankets.
- The biggest danger with transporting a mammal is escape. Many mammals can chew their way out of a cardboard box or plastic crate in just a few minutes. Make sure the container used is secure enough to confine the animal.

Chapter 5

POST CAPTURE–
WHAT NOW?

O nce an animal is captured, the best possible outcome would be its immediate transportation to a wildlife veterinarian or rehabilitator. If you have prepared in advance and have the phone number with you, contacting them would be your next step.

Be prepared to transport the animal yourself. Most rehabilitators work on a volunteer basis with very limited funds. Many do not have the resources to pick up animals and need your assistance to get that animal into the rehabilitation system.

If you do not have the contact information handy or if there is no immediate answer, you may have to hold the animal for a short time.

TRANSPORTATION

At some point you will have to transport the animal either to the rehabilitator or to your home for temporary holding. This sounds easy and, with a little common sense, it is. How the animal is transported will have a great effect on the animal's stress level. The following guidelines will help reduce the animal's anxiety during the ride.

- Be safe traveling. Don't allow excitement and adrenaline to take over. Follow the speed limits and obey all the traffic laws. You can't help the animal if you are injured in an accident.
- Keep the animal in the dark and remove any visual stimulation. If the animal is in a cardboard box, this has already been accomplished. If the animal can see out, cover the container completely with a towel, blanket, or coat.

- The best place to position the box for transport is on the floor behind the front passenger's or driver's seat. If this is not possible, place the box as centrally located in the vehicle as possible. This will lessen movement when turning and driving over rough roadways. If possible, secure the container by tying it down to prevent rolling.
- *Do not* transport animals in the trunk or in the open bed of a pickup.
- *Do not* play the radio. Music may be soothing to you but is completely foreign to a wild animal. Dark and quiet are the keys to a stress-free trip.
- *Do not* smoke. Just as the radio may be a stress factor, the smell of smoke can intensify an animal's feeling of danger. Think of all possible causes of stress and try to eliminate them during the ride.
- Avoid the temptation to peek. Animals often calm down and become quiet during transport, and you may fear that the creature is getting worse or has expired. A slight opening of the container may be all the animal needs to encourage an escape attempt, and you do not want the animal loose in your car.

TEMPORARY HOLDING

It may be necessary to house the animal temporarily until contact with a rehabilitator can be made. This is a critical time during the rescue process, and often people make the worst mistakes by trying to help the animal. This is when people often try to feed the animal, examine it, and begin critical care. These steps often result in a worsening condition of the animal, a complication of its situation, or even death.

What the animal needs during this time is warmth, darkness, and quiet.

Again, avoiding the temptation to peek, place the box in an unused spare bedroom or bathroom and close the door. Keep everyone, especially children and pets, away from the animal.

If the animal is very young, you may need to supply supplemental heat to keep it warm. Placing a heating pad set on *low* under half

You Need a Box

A gentleman called one afternoon asking for directions to the center. He was driving on a highway when he witnessed a turkey vulture get hit by the car in front of him. The bird had been dining on a road-killed deer and was slow to get out of the way of the traffic. The vulture was unconscious but still breathing. Identifying his location, I gave him directions to a local market. There he could get a box in which to place the bird and write down the directions to our center. He stated that he had no time—the bird needed immediate care—and asked if I could remain on the phone and talk him through the directions. "You need to stop and get a box," I insisted, but he assured me the bird was safe in the back seat, and he did not want to stop.

I watched down the road from the center's window as I listened over the phone to the man ranting about the uncaring driver who "didn't even stop to see if the bird was injured." Soon I saw his new red sports car winding down our country road. I was talking him through the last turn and into the driveway when I noticed what looked like a large bird perched behind the driver. I calmly told him to pull into the driveway,

exit the vehicle immediately, and *don't look in the mirror.* My words unheeded, the man screamed, and I feared he was going to drive straight into the window where I was standing. He managed to get his car stopped before scrambling and falling out of the vehicle. I heard more screaming over the phone as he lay in my driveway and quickly kicked the car door shut.

Vultures are scavenging birds and eat carrion. They can locate a meal by smelling the gases given off by rotting flesh from up to three miles away. By the time a vulture finds this delicacy, the stench from the meat is extremely strong. They are capable of ingesting large quantities of this tenderized meal, often eating so much that they have difficulty flying. Because they are not swift birds, cannot flee quickly, have no vocal cords to emit a warning scream, and no obvious defensive tools other than a sharp beak, one might believe these birds to be defenseless. The opposite is true, however, as these birds have a repugnant ability to regurgitate their latest meal (which is accompanied by strong stomach acid) and fling it at an attacker. The odor is noxious and lasting, often difficult to remove.

Morrie Katz with Hannibal the turkey vulture

Wearing gloves and a face shield, I carefully entered the car, approaching the bird that had fully awakened from its recent head trauma. I talked gently and moved slowly so as to not frighten the bird further, but the drama was too much for him. The vulture began to pump his head, and his highway meal came to the surface. The bird shook his head, and the entire interior of the brand-new BMW sports car became splattered with partially digested roadkill. The sludge dripped off the windows and ran down the suede leather seats. Gagging from the smell, I wrapped the bird in a blanket and removed him from the car.

The man called a week later to inquire about the bird. He was relieved to hear that it had suffered no fractures and was about to be released. I inquired about his vehicle, and he laughed. He had agreed to turn the car over to his ex-wife as part of a renegotiated divorce settlement. He was having the car delivered to her that evening.

Pet Owners Beware

If you have pets in your home, be aware that they can contract many diseases and parasites common in wildlife. This is especially true if you own pet birds. You do not want your attempt at rescuing a wild animal to result in the loss of a beloved pet.

If you have pets in your home, you may not wish to bring a wild animal inside at all. Housing it temporarily on an outside porch or in a garage may be a safer choice to protect your pets.

To ensure that cross-contamination does not occur, it is advisable to shower and change clothing before handling any susceptible pets, and discard anything that came in contact with the wild animal.

of the container will allow the animal to move toward or away from the heat to regulate its own body temperature.

If a heating pad is not available, a hot water bottle or soda bottle filled with warm water and placed inside a sock can be a comfortable heat source for the animal to snuggle against.

In most cases, do not attempt to feed the animal.

It is a basic human instinct to feed an animal to comfort it, especially when it comes to baby animals. However, food is the last thing most animals need when in distress. In the case of an injured animal or one suffering from dehydration, food can kill that animal.

An animal that has suffered injury, exposure, and lack of food for any length of time will also be suffering from dehydration. If dehydrated, fluids must be stabilized first or the animal will not be able to process food at all. If it eats, the food often lays in the stomach or crop and decomposes without being digested, which complicates its condition.

If you were in a car accident, had suffered cuts, bruises, and fractures, and an ambulance crew came to your aid, *they would not feed you.*

Once you reached the hospital, you would be examined and medicated and you would receive I.V. fluids, but *they would not feed you.*

If you needed surgery, you may receive more fluids, possibly blood, and more medication. And, when you woke up, *they would not feed you.*

Just like a human trauma case, an injured animal needs first to be stabilized and rehydrated. Food is then gradually introduced, often initially in the form of a liquid diet. Rushing this important step can be just enough to push a compromised animal over the edge.

EXCEPTIONS TO THE "DO NOT FEED" RULE

Of course, for every rule there is an exception. With animals, that exception is *very tiny birds.*

Hummingbirds

Hummingbirds have an extremely high metabolism, and if their feeding intervals are interrupted or extended they can shut down rather quickly. Hummingbirds need to eat every fifteen to thirty minutes during daylight hours. Even when they are injured, they still need to eat continuously.

Hummingbirds can be offered a drink by dipping their beak into a hummingbird feeder, or they can be fed from a dropper. Offer nectar or sugar water (one quarter cup of sugar dissolved into one cup of water) every fifteen to twenty minutes.

If using a dropper, do not squeeze out the nectar. Placing the very tip of the beak in the nectar should be enough to encourage the bird to drink on its own. It is a wondrous thing to watch a hummingbird drink, as their tongue will quickly flick in and out as the nectar volume decreases. If the hummingbird can perch or remain upright on its own, making the nectar available at all times will keep the bird hydrated and stable until transport can be arranged.

Baby Songbirds

Tiny baby birds such as sparrows and finches also cannot survive long without hydration and calories. Hand-feeding these baby birds can be quite dangerous, as too much food or the wrong liquidity can result in aspiration.

It's a Rabbit—It's a Squirrel—It's . . .

"Hello, Red Creek. May I help you?"

"Hi. I have a wildlife situation. There's a baby rabbit, well maybe it's a squirrel, but it's in my yard and I don't want it to die there."

"It would help if I knew which it was. Baby squirrels have long tails and long legs, and rabbits do not."

"Well, that's the problem. I think its mother rejected it because it has birth defects. It does have really long back legs but doesn't have any tail at all. It doesn't have ears either. It also doesn't have any fur yet and its front legs are deformed."

"Deformed?"

"Yes. The front legs are all shriveled and gnarly and useless. It'll never hop or climb a tree. I'm sure that's why the mother got rid of it, but I don't want to watch it die in my yard! And I think it's suffering because it looks like it's trying to scream but no sound comes out. Can you just put it to sleep?"

I asked the woman to bring me the squirrelly rabbit, and when I opened the box, I removed a perfectly formed, perfectly healthy . . . baby bird.

It was a hatchling. At this age they are ugly, no more than a large digestive system with long legs and stubby little wings. Those gnarly front legs were the wings that would one day carry him high into the

Baby birds must be supported and kept in a tight, nestlike container. This can be achieved by placing tissues in an appropriately sized berry box, margarine container, or small bowl. If baby birds are kept on a flat or slippery surface, the legs may spread, causing injury or deformity.

If you need to keep a baby bird for a few hours, first make sure the bird is warm and active before attempting to introduce anything by mouth. Stabilize the bird's body temperature by placing half the box on a heating pad set on *low*. If the nestling is still chilled, drop a tissue over top of the bird to help maintain its warmth.

sky. The baby bird weakly opened its mouth, begging for food.

"See there! It's trying to scream!"

As I offered it a paintbrush dipped in hand-feeding formula, I explained that it was a bird. The bird ate hungrily and begged for more. Since it was healthy and unharmed, this bird would have been a good candidate for renesting. Normally, I would have sent the bird back with the finder along with a wicker basket and instructions on how to reintroduce the bird to its parents. I looked at the woman, who was dumbfounded by this new knowledge; I grabbed an intake sheet instead.

According to my permit requirements, I must record each animal we receive along with complete contact information for the person who brings the animal. In the area for species, I wrote "European starling." For the woman, I recorded her name, address, phone number, and the planet from which she came.

The first offerings should be small drops of liquid for the purpose of increasing hydration. Pedialyte or Gatorade mixed half-and-half with water will do. If these are unavailable, you can boil plain, non-diet cola to remove the carbonation and mix half-and-half with water.

Tiny portions given every few minutes will increase hydration while reducing the chances of aspiration or drowning. A small, hobby paintbrush is a simple tool that works quite well for delivering a single drop of liquid at a time.

Most baby birds can be encouraged to open their beaks for you. Sometimes tapping lightly on the container (simulating a mother

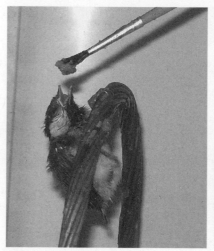

Dry kitten food soaked in water makes a good emergency meal.

landing on the nest) will trigger a feeding response. With the mouth open (called "gaping"), place one drop at a time as far back into the mouth as possible.

If the baby will not gape, *do not* force-feed the bird—some birds, such as doves, do not eat in this manner.

If the baby bird needs to be kept for longer than a few hours, you may need to begin feeding the bird. For almost all songbird species, dry kitten food is an excellent temporary replacement. Soak the dry kitten food in water until soft, then mix to a puddinglike texture.

Dab a small paintbrush in the mixture and place it at the back of the bird's throat behind the glottis or airway.

Using the paintbrush, pick up small amounts of the kitten food and place far back into the gaping mouth. Wait for the bird to swallow before offering more food. Small amounts fed every fifteen minutes will increase its strength and supply the energy it needs until transport can be arranged.

Please be aware that these directions are for **temporary emergency care only.**

These directions do not supply the necessary nutrition for proper growth and development and are only intended to keep a small bird alive until transport to a licensed rehabilitator can be arranged.

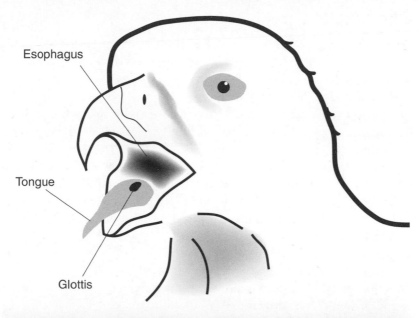

Esophagus

Tongue

Glottis

Food should be placed behind the bird's glottis, which is located at the back of the tongue.

CLEANUP

Once the emergency is over, and the animal is back in the environment or with a rehabilitator, be sure to clean and disinfect everything with which the animal came in contact. This is especially important if you have other pets or small children.

If you used a cardboard box for capture and transport, it should be discarded or burned. Any bedding you used should also be discarded.

If you used pet carriers or another container you wish to keep, all urine, blood, and fecal matter should first be removed with detergent. Hydrogen peroxide is excellent for removing blood. Rinse thoroughly and be sure all organic matter has been removed, because organic material cannot be properly disinfected.

Once clean, you are ready to disinfect. Dilute one part chlorine bleach with ten parts water and thoroughly drench the surface with the solution. Allow it to remain wet for at least ten or more minutes before rinsing. Then allow it to dry.

You should also shower and launder your clothing to remove any parasites and other contaminants.

Chapter 6
EMERGENCY CARE

ALLEVIATE LIFE-THREATENING CONDITIONS

I am not recommending performing first aid on any animal, but there are a few life-threatening conditions that may cause the animal to die before transportation can be accomplished if not immediately corrected. There are life-threatening conditions such as bleeding, airway obstruction, or hypo- or hyperthermia that you may be able to safely alleviate. These conditions can be quickly determined with a cursory glance and do not require a close physical examination.

Again, as always, your safety and the safety of the animal are your primary concerns. When presented with a life-threatening condition, it is important to work quickly and efficiently to avoid unnecessary handling and additional stress.

Follow the ABCs:

Airway
Breathing
Circulation (heartbeat and severe bleeding)

Airway and Breathing

1. If the animal has an obstructed airway, attempt to remove the obstruction.

Heimlich Maneuver
Hold a small animal upright or put a large animal on its side. Apply force/pressure with fingers or fist just below the sternum

in an upward motion (toward the head) quickly, five times. Repeat as necessary.

Remove any visible obstructions
   a. Do *not* put your fingers into the mouth of an animal.
   b. If animal is unconscious and you can see the foreign object in the throat, attempt to remove it with long forceps or a similar instrument.
   c. Be careful to not push the obstruction down farther.
2. Discharge can be wiped out of the mouth or nostrils with a swab or suctioned out with an eyedropper or turkey baster.
3. Reposition the head so the airway is open.
4. Any "sucking" wounds (punctures that have entered the airway or respiratory system) can be sealed with an airtight bandage, such as plastic wrap and gauze taped tightly to the area.

Bleeding
1. Apply direct pressure with a gauze pad to any bleeding wound(s)
   a. Do not remove the cloth.
   b. If blood soaks the material, add another layer on top.
   c. A bandage may be wrapped around the cloth and taped in place.
2. **Blood feathers** are new, growing feathers that still have a blood supply in the vein. If broken or torn, these feathers will bleed profusely.
   a. Apply direct pressure by squeezing the feather shaft closed. The bleeding should stop quickly.
   b. Do not attempt to pull blood feathers out, as this procedure can be painful and dangerous to the bird and should be left to a professional.

Hypothermia (low body temperature)
Lack of calories, shock, and exposure can result in low body temperature. Many young animals are not self-regulating and cannot produce their own body heat. Signs of hypothermia include shivering, sluggishness, dull or slow response to stimuli, shallow breathing, and

coma. Infant animals may not show all the signs because of an undeveloped reflex response. Supplying supplemental heat will help stabilize the patient before it reaches the rehabilitation center or veterinarian.

Efforts must be made to warm an animal without overheating or burning it. Supplemental heat in the field can be obtained by using instant hand warmers, or by filling a soda or water bottle with warm water and placing it inside a sock or wrapping it in a t-shirt. Allow the animal to snuggle up to the warmth, leaving it enough room to move away should it become too warm.

If the animal cannot be immediately transported to the rehabilitation center or veterinarian, maintain a source of heat by placing a heating pad under the container. Set the heating pad on *low* and position half of the box over the pad so the animal can move away from the heat source.

Hyperthermia (heatstroke)

The opposite of hypothermia is hyperthermia, or overheating. Baby animals that have been exposed to the elements are often cold and sluggish. Occasionally, that infant animal will lie helplessly in the sun and actually bake. We have had people find cold animals and place them under heating lamps or on heating pads hoping to warm the animal before calling us, essentially "cooking" the animal. If the animal has been exposed to extreme heat and the body feels hot, it must be cooled to avoid organ and neurological damage.

- Overheated animals should *not* be doused with cold water.
- Cover with cool, wet towels for transport and/or bathe in tepid water to help bring body temperature down.
- Rubbing alcohol applied to the footpads can also help.

Tars and Glue

Many animals are presented to us after having been stuck on flypaper or on a rodent glue-board. Others come in covered with tar or another sticky substance such as pine sap. Animals can also be found stuck in fresh tar on a roof or driveway.

A Bundle of Squirrels

Wildlife conservation officers (or game wardens, as they used to be called in Pennsylvania) are often portrayed as hard-hearted and uncaring when it concerns individual animals. I've often found this to be completely untrue, such as when an officer presented me with a bundle of baby squirrels.

Collective groups of animals often have unusual names, such as a "murder" of crows or a "paddling" of ducks. Groups of squirrels are correctly called a "dray" or "scurry" of squirrels, but on this early April morning they were a bundle, because the four squirrels in front of me had their tails firmly glued together!

The officer who rescued them was angry. "Someone glued the squirrels' tails together! Had to be kids to do such a thing! When I find out who they are, I'm throwing the book at them!"

As the officer described the neighborhood park where they were found, I removed the squirrels from the box. They were about six weeks old—too young to be without mom but old enough to be exploring their new world. At this age they would still be nursing but would also be taste-testing new things. Their teeth were coming in.

The squirrels were in a panic and trying to escape, but since each was trying to run in a different direction, they couldn't go anywhere. As a result, the tails were not just glued, but were firmly tied in knots. The babies looked otherwise healthy, well-fed and not injured or dehydrated.

Together, we tried to control the squirrels while examining the tails. My fingers were becoming sticky with the glue, and suddenly I realized what had happened.

The previous day had been untypically warm for April, warm enough for pine-tree sap to liquefy. The baby squirrels had probably scampered and played during the warm day, returning to a pine tree in the evening to sleep for the night. Curled up together in the nook of the pine branches, they may have bedded down too close to a pool of soft sap, and their tails absorbed the liquid like small paintbrushes. As the babies slept, the sap hardened in the cool air of the night and glued their tails

together. As I began pulling pine needles from the mat of tail fur, my suspicions were confirmed.

I reached for a bottle of mineral oil and began carefully working it into the tails. Suddenly the squirrels, now free of each other, began to bolt in different directions in the room—leaving trails of oily pine tar behind them.

Grabbing nets, we captured each one and cleaned the oil and remaining tar from the fur. Their agility was remarkable, and I knew it wouldn't be long until they would be independent, jumping through tree branches like trapeze artists.

They growled and objected every step of the way as the officer returned them to the park and their family. As he released them, they must have recognized home. Each ran with no concept of direction for a bit, then turned and scampered up the trunk of a huge pine tree in the center of the park.

This type of emergency needs immediate intervention before the animal is even moved. If left untreated, the animal's struggles will ensnare it further, exposing more of its skin to the substance and possibly blocking its airway. In an effort to clean itself, the animal may ingest some of the product, possibly resulting in poisoning.

Do not attempt to pull the animal loose. This will injure the animal further, not only destroying feathers and fur, but also tearing the skin and causing tremendous pain and stress.

Do not use harsh chemicals to try to remove the glue or tar. Instead, you want to coat the substance with a light, safe oil such as cooking oil or mineral oil. This will immediately stop the adhesive effect and protect the animal from further involvement.

If the animal is stuck on a paper or board that can be moved, all you need to do is to coat the board or paper with the oil (not the animal) and transport the animal that way. The oil covering on the trap will render the rest of the glue harmless.

If the animal is covered in a sticky substance such as tar, lightly coat the animal itself on the areas involved to keep the animal from sticking to itself and the transport box.

An animal that is caught in the tar on a roof or roadway must be removed before transport. To safely remove the animal, follow these instructions:

- For animals that are capable of biting, scratching, or injuring you once free, protect yourself from bites and scratches by wearing heavy leather gloves.
- For other animals, it's best to wear latex or rubber gloves when possible to keep the ensuing mess off your own skin.
- Drench a clean paintbrush, cotton swab, or paper towel with cooking oil or mineral oil and slowly work the oil between the animal and the sticky surface.
- Keep refilling the brush and work slowly to ensure that fur, feathers, and skin are not torn loose. Do not pull. The oil will liquefy the tar, but it does take a little bit of time and patience. *Work slowly.*
- As the animal is worked free, be ready to wrap it in a towel or rag to soak up the extra oil.

- Place the animal in a box with paper towels and transport it as soon as possible.

Even if the unstuck animal seems fine and is completely free, it should still be taken to a rehabilitation center. The oil needs to be safely removed from the animal, and the creature also needs to be observed for a few days for toxic effects from possible ingestion of and exposure to the adhesive.

Chapter 7
MORE INFORMATION

WHAT IS RABIES?

Rabies is a fatal disease caused by a virus that attacks the central nervous system of warm-blooded animals. All mammals can get rabies, including pets, livestock, and humans. The most commonly affected animals are raccoons, skunks, foxes, bats, and domestic cats.

The rabies virus travels slowly via the nervous system until it reaches the brain. In most species, the time from infection to disease is two to twelve weeks, but some animals have been known to carry the virus for up to a year. Once the virus reaches the brain and clinical signs appear, death follows in two weeks or less. This is also when the virus reaches the saliva and can infect others through exposure. In most animals (bats are an exception), the virus is only transmissible during this last stage of the disease. Once this last stage is reached, rabies is *always* fatal.

Rabies is most often contracted through a bite or scratch, but it can also be transmitted when the saliva or brain tissue of an infected animal comes in contact with an open cut or mucous membranes such as the eyes.

Clinical signs in wild animals can vary greatly and should not be used to judge whether or not an animal is rabid. Some common signs are changes in normal behavior, unnatural friendliness or aggression, foaming at the mouth, blindness, and paralysis. Some animals, however, die with no visible signs.

Extra precautions *must* be taken with animals that are known to carry rabies in your area. If you think you have had a possible exposure, seek medical advice from your doctor immediately or call your state's department of health. It will instruct you on the steps necessary to protect your health and have the animal tested for rabies.

TWENTY WAYS TO HELP WILDLIFE EVERY DAY

1. *Keep cats and dogs inside!* Roaming pets are the number-one cause of injury to baby wildlife.
2. Do not feed wildlife. Attracting large numbers of animals to any given area can hasten the spread of diseases, including rabies (see 19).
3. Teach your children to respect wildlife and emphasize a hands-off policy. This includes nests and eggs.
4. Adjust mower blades to their highest level. Walk the area to be mowed and check for rabbit nests (these are very difficult to spot). If you do know of a nest, mark it and mow around it. In less than two weeks, the nest will be empty.
5. Do birds fly into your windows? Hang a silhouette of a hawk in the window, place vertical pinstripes on the window, or leave the windows "dirty" to reduce reflection.
6. Place bird feeders away from shrubs where cats can hide.
7. Dispose of garbage properly and cut all six-pack rings so wildlife cannot get entangled.
8. Remove fishing line from ponds and streams. Abandoned hooks, line, and lures are deadly to waterfowl.

Rabies on the Roadway

I enjoy continuing education classes; I always learn something new. The information I had learned during one such class on rabies was very disturbing: *A significantly higher percentage of roadkill raccoons test positive for rabies than a general sampling of the population.*

Not quite sure why this was the case, the speaker hypothesized that, in their crazed state, raccoons may be attracted to the sounds of cars. The implications of this were horrifying.

While a compromised animal found elsewhere may give a person pause about the reason for the animal's distress, it is easy for one to assume an injured raccoon on the roadway is a healthy animal compromised by an accident. Precautions might be overlooked in cases of trauma, but, with this information, we need to ask, "Why was that raccoon on the road in the first place?" Over a year later, I witnessed, quite by accident, this phenomenon for myself.

I had delivered a large owl to Kutztown Animal Hospital and was on my way home. The road before me was a four-lane highway ascending a hill. The north- and southbound lanes were divided by a cement "jersey wall." The light turned yellow, then red as I approached the intersection of routes 61 and 895.

As I sat at the red light, cars entered the roadway from my right and began climbing the hill. I noticed the cars were swerving and slowing down. A large raccoon was in the roadway, running about erratically and chasing the cars. One car stopped, and the raccoon ran up and bit at a tire.

I took a quick mental inventory of the equipment I had in the van. I had a large dog carrier that had transported the owl. I had gloves and a single bedsheet that had covered the crate. I had no net or rabies catch pole, and I was alone. This was going to be tough. When the light turned green, I put on my four-way flashers and drove up the hill.

Parking on the shoulder, I lifted the tailgate of the van and opened the carrier. Grabbing the gloves and sheet, I turned just as a car veered off, barely missing me and the van. Other cars were approaching and, in an attempt to miss the raccoon, swerving randomly. I motioned with my arms for the cars to slow down, but their attention seemed to be on the raccoon. I feared I was going to get hit.

The light at the intersection changed again, and I watched the traffic. Cars entering the intersection were turning south, and a large tractor trailer was facing north waiting for the green. I had a window of opportunity and ran toward the raccoon. With only a bedsheet and gloves for protection, I was afraid the raccoon would now turn on me, but it started running away along the jersey wall. I ran up behind the raccoon, threw the sheet over it, and missed.

Suddenly, the sound of the tractor trailer was behind me. I turned to look, and the truck pulled along the wall and turned sharply toward the shoulder. The truck stopped, blocking both lanes and the shoulder. The driver exited the truck and began to climb down.

"Get back in the truck—he's RABID!" I ordered.

"YOU'RE NUTS, LADY!" he yelled back.

The raccoon now turned and headed toward the truck. I remembered the speaker saying how the sounds of automobiles could attract rabid raccoons. That appeared to be the case as the raccoon, ignoring me, ran right past me and toward the tractor trailer. I threw the sheet a second time, successfully dropping it over his head. He stumbled into the sheet.

Grabbing the sheet and the raccoon's tail, I haphazardly twisted the sheet around him as I ran toward the van. The raccoon writhed and snarled but was entangled enough that its struggles were in vain. I shoved the raccoon and sheet into the crate and slammed the door. The raccoon collapsed inside the crate. On inspection, the raccoon's legs were covered with self-inflicted bite wounds—another common sign of rabies in raccoons.

The choices I made that day were deliberate and should not be repeated by members of the public. I knew there was a clear possibility of being injured by the raccoon or hit by a vehicle, but I also knew that the raccoon would have soon been hit and, if not killed, may have been rescued by someone who had no idea of the animal's state of health. I was at least partially equipped and vaccinated for rabies.

With a thank you and a business card, the truck driver went on his way, and the traffic flowed freely once more. The raccoon was euthanized and tested for rabies, which came back positive. At least the disease was prevented from spreading, and the raccoon was spared one last day of suffering.

9. Don't use pesticides on your lawn, and avoid using chemicals outside your home.
10. Dispose of oil and antifreeze properly. If your car has a fluid leak, clean it up immediately.
11. Be alert when driving in rural areas, and especially if you see an animal dead on the road. Many animals such as opossums, crows, and hawks will scavenge for food and may become roadkill themselves.
12. Place caps on chimneys and screens on dryer vents to keep out birds and raccoons.
13. Check trees for nests or dens before cutting or trimming. Leave hollow trunks standing as natural nesting sights.
14. Don't use glue traps and flypaper outdoors, in barns, or in attics. You may catch birds and bats.
15. Before starting vehicles that have been parked for a period of time, check for animals nesting in the engine compartment.
16. Wash all bird feeders once a week with a solution of one part bleach to thirty parts water. This helps prevent the spread of diseases such as conjunctivitis, a very contagious eye infection.
17. Move turtles off the road but *do not* relocate them. Box turtles thrive *only* in their immediate, original habitat.
18. Leave baby animals alone. If you think an animal is in distress, call your local wildlife rehabilitator *before* interfering. What you are witnessing may be normal behavior.
19. Provide habitat for wildlife by planting gardens and naturalizing your property (see 2).
20. Support your local wildlife rehabilitator.

WHAT IS IMPRINTING?

Most mammals and birds recognize their own species through a process called "imprinting." When an animal is very young and its eyes begin to focus, it looks at who is nurturing, feeding, and protecting it. From this individual, the young animal gets a mental picture of who is caring for it. This picture (or imprint) stays with the animal its entire life and, once formed, cannot be changed.

Exactly when this happens depends on the species. Ducks and geese, for example, imprint almost immediately, and this is reinforced during the first weeks of life. A great horned owl's eyes begin to focus at about two weeks of age. Imprinting takes place shortly thereafter. Mammal eyes open and focus at various stages of their development.

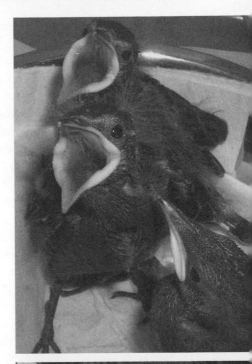

This imprint not only gives an animal its identity, it also serves to help it choose a mate later in life. This is why a blue bird doesn't attempt to mate with a blue jay, or a red fox with a gray fox. The wrong species doesn't match that imprint. An animal is looking for a mate "just like mom."

Most of the time this works quite well: Geese raise geese, crows raise crows, and deer raise deer. But when a person hand-raises a wild animal, that animal can grow up believing it is a person. It will seek out people when it wants company, is injured or scared, and when it's time to mate.

It is a very miserable life for an animal that is imprinted on humans. It faces a life of frustration and rejection. Just think what it would be like if you were physically incompatible with everyone to whom you were attracted.

Even if the animal is past the age of imprinting and learns to accept humans, without others of its species with which to interact, it never learns the proper etiquette of behaving around other animals. An animal that doesn't use the proper body language and behavior will be rejected by other members of its own species.

Wildlife rehabilitators deal with the problems of imprinting in numerous ways, some of which are described below.

Surrogates. Wildlife rehabilitators often have a selection of non-releasable adult animals that can serve as foster parents for orphaned babies. The babies grow up with a natural parent, learning proper behavior and the skills they will need to survive.

Strength in numbers. Because wildlife rehabilitators receive large numbers of animals from the surrounding area, baby animals don't have to grow up alone. They are placed with other babies of their species who are in the same situation. Together they grow and bond and learn to interact. Once old enough to be released, they are released together as a family unit.

Rehabilitator networks. Wildlife rehabilitators network with one another. If a rehabilitator receives a single baby, it can be placed with another rehabilitator who has others of that species.

CATS VERSUS WILDLIFE

How Many Cats Are There in the United States?

According to the most recently documented statistics, the estimated number of pet cats in urban and rural regions of the United States has grown from 30 million in 1970 to 88 million in 2008. These estimates included only those cats that people claim to "own" as pets, not cats that are semi-wild or free-ranging. Nationwide, approximately 34 percent of households have at least one cat. In rural areas where free-ranging cats are usually not regarded as pets, approximately 60 percent of households have cats.

What Effects do Domestics Cats Have on Wildlife?

Although rural cats take the greatest toll on wildlife, even urban house pets take live prey when allowed outside. Small mammals make up approximately 70 percent of these cats' prey, while birds make up about 20 percent. The remaining 10 percent is a variety of other animals.

Observation of free-ranging domestic cats shows that some individuals can kill over one thousand wild animals per year. Nationwide, rural cats probably kill over a billion small mammals and hundreds of millions of birds each year. Urban and suburban cats add to this toll. Some of these kills are house mice, rats, and other species considered pests, but many are native songbirds and mammals whose populations are already stressed by other factors such as habitat destruction and pesticide pollution.

Worldwide, cats may have been involved in the extinction of more bird species than any other factor except habitat destruction. Cats are contributing to the endangerment of populations of birds such as least terns, piping plovers, and loggerhead shrikes. In Key West, Florida, marsh rabbits have been threatened by predation from domestic cats. Cats introduced by people living on the barrier islands of Florida's coast have depleted several unique species of mice and woodrats to near extinction.

The Effect on Native Predators

Not only do cats prey on many small mammals and birds, they can also outnumber and compete with native predators. Domestic cats eat many of the same animals as native predators. When present in large numbers, cats can reduce the availability of prey for native predators, such as hawks. Free-ranging domestic cats may also transmit new diseases to wild animals. Domestic cats have spread feline leukemia virus to mountain lions and may have recently infected the endangered Florida panther with feline panleukopenia (commonly known as feline distemper, an immune deficiency disease). These diseases may pose a serious threat to these rare species. Some free-ranging domestic cats also carry several diseases that are easily transmitted to humans, including rabies and toxoplasmosis, a parasitic disease that usually causes flulike symptoms. In more serious cases, toxoplasmosis can cause inflammation of the brain and affect the heart, liver, and eyes.

Because many cats are protected and fed by humans, their population is not checked by natural occurrences such as disease, predation, and scarcity of wild game.

The Effect on Cats

The average life span of an indoor house cat is about fifteen years. A free-roaming domestic cat can expect to live only between one and two years. This is due to disease, injuries, infection resulting from fights with wild animals and other cats, and automobile accidents. Domestic cats are also one of the favored foods of the eastern coyote and the great horned owl. Keeping a cat indoors protects local wildlife as well as the cat and the people with whom the cat comes in contact.

Even young great horned owls can pose a danger to cats.

The Effect on People

Rabies is a virus that attacks the central nervous system of warm-blooded animals, including humans. Once it reaches the final symptomatic stage, it is 100 percent fatal. Cats are one of the most common carriers of rabies, and many rural cats are not vaccinated. Because of their close association with people and other domestic animals, cats pose a greater risk of transmitting rabies to humans and other pets than do wild rabies vector species such as raccoons, skunks, foxes, woodchucks, coyotes, and bats.

How You Can Help

People who own pet cats
- Keep only as many pets as you can control and care for.
- Keep domestic cats indoors.
- Spay and neuter all cats.
- Vaccinate all cats regularly.
- Place bird feeders away from areas where cats can hide and stalk birds.
- Leash-train your cat for outdoor exercise.

Farmers who need barnyard cats for rodent control
- Keep only as many cats as needed to control rodent populations.
- Spay and neuter all cats. Spayed female cats are more likely to stay close to farm buildings.
- Vaccinate all cats regularly.
- Place owl boxes near barns to attract natural predators.

FEEDING WILDLIFE

Do you enjoy watching wildlife "up close and personal?" Most people who feed wildlife do so because they love animals and enjoy the interaction. Feeding wildlife becomes a regular hobby, and the hobbyist believes that the animals benefit from the experience.

Feeding wildlife is actually destructive and dangerous for the wild animals that are being fed. People who feed wildlife do not realize the danger in which they are actually placing the animals. The loving act of feeding wildlife becomes a selfish love where the only one who truly benefits is the person doing the feeding.

Overpopulation

The number of young a pair of animals produces is in direct proportion to the amount of food available. When food is unnaturally added to an area, the animals will overpopulate that area very quickly. Once overpopulated, animals will compete for a limited number of nesting areas. When natural nesting areas aren't available, the animals invade houses and other buildings, becoming a nuisance.

Habitat Contamination

When large numbers of animals habituate an area, that area can become contaminated quickly with feces, which fosters disease and bacteria. Nature, however, balances itself very well. A particular habitat has only enough food for a certain number of animals. Once that food supply is gone, the animals will move to a new habitat *before* the ground becomes saturated to the point of becoming unhealthy. Once the animals have left, the earth cleans itself through enzymes and microbial activity, and a new food supply grows. The rejuvenated habitat can once again support wildlife and the animals return, starting the cycle over.

A classic example of this pertains to ducks and geese. Botulism—a paralytic bacteria-produced illness—often develops on the bottom of ponds and lakes when the number of birds in the area is unnaturally high due to supplemental feeding. A strong rain on a hot summer day will bring the contaminants to the surface, causing entire flocks of birds to be affected and die.

Spread of Disease

Diseases in wildlife are kept in check because animals usually do not associate with each other closely in the wild. These diseases will spread rapidly through animals who gather near a food supply. Rabies and distemper can spread among mammals simply by their eating from the same dishes. Mammals are not the only animals affected. Avian conjunctivitis is an extremely contagious eye infection that affects songbirds, especially sparrows. This disease is easily spread by birds gathering and sharing food at bird feeders.

Nutrition

Animals who routinely eat an unnatural diet often suffer from dietary problems. Foods commonly fed to them by people are often nutritionally inadequate. In infants and juveniles, growth and developmental problems result in crippling deformities that are often fatal. Adults can suffer from digestive problems, serious health conditions, and behavioral disturbances.

Safety

Another reason to avoid feeding wildlife is to ensure they retain their fear of humans. *You* may not pose a threat to their survival, but if they do not fear *all* humans, they are bound to encounter an unfriendly one sooner or later.

So What Can You Do?

You can enjoy wildlife visiting your backyard with some positive changes. Instead of supplying food, supply *habitat*: an increasingly limited commodity.

In today's ever-changing world, habitat loss is the number-one reason for distressed wildlife. Planned landscaping that includes the addition of natural food-bearing plants as well as nesting and hiding places will attract wildlife without disrupting their natural routines.

For example, hummingbird feeders supply energy with no nutrition. Leaving a hummingbird feeder out too late in the season can "trap" them in an area after migration. Planting nectar-producing flowers will attract hummingbirds to your garden, supplying them with nutritionally rich foods that will disappear when it is time for the birds to migrate.

WILD PETS

People who find animals can be very tempted to raise them or keep them as pets. There is a multitude of reasons why this is *not* a wise decision.

We've already covered the many risks to you, your family, and your pets through contact with wildlife. Keeping wildlife in your home for any period of time increases these risks each day that you share your home with a wild animal. I've also touched on the emotional damage the animal suffers through imprinting (see page 104).

In addition, wild animals need special, experienced care. They require specific nutrition, medical attention, and housing.

Milk Formulas for Baby Animals

We are often presented with baby animals after people have fed milk to them for days or weeks before bringing them to us. Often these babies are suffering digestive distress and malnutrition. Before you attempt to feed milk to a baby animal, please consider the complexity involved.

Each species of animal has different nutritional requirements for proper development including the fat/protein ratio of their milk. Milk designed for cats (carnivores, or meat-eaters) is high in protein so the kitten can develop strong bones and muscles more slowly. Rabbits (herbivores, or plant-eaters) need high fat content to grow very quickly and do not need the high protein of a carnivore diet. Thus, feeding kitten milk to rabbits (which we often see suggested on various websites) is incorrect.

Aside from having the right milk formulation, the correct amount needs to be fed at proper intervals. Most baby animals' stomach capacity is a percentage of their body weight and thus varies by

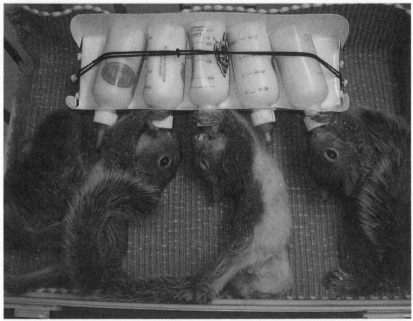

Baby squirrels need a special milk formulation to grow strong.

These squirrels are the same age, but the one in the center was fed Similac for five days by the person who found it. That baby eventually died.

Can I Keep It?

When you are tempted to take a wild animal home as a pet, ask yourself the following questions:

- Is what I am doing legal?
- Am I willing to risk the health, and possibly the lives, of myself, my family, and our pets?
- Am I properly trained in the care of this species of animal?
- Can I obtain veterinary care for this animal? (Veterinarians will not treat wildlife possessed unlawfully.)
- Am I willing to risk killing the animal because I may not truly know how to care for it?
- Am I willing to change my lifestyle to conform to the animal's natural and unalterable behavior?

    If you cannot truthfully answer yes to *every* question, please do not attempt to keep a wild animal as a pet.

species. Babies must be weighed daily to determine the proper serving amounts. If the wrong amount is given, the animal becomes a victim of either diarrhea (from too much) or starvation (from too little). Caloric intake must also be monitored to make sure the animal has the energy to grow properly. The calculation for a baby mammal is: $70 \times W^{.75} \times S = Kcals/24$ hours (W = weight in kilograms) (S = stress factor). The stress factor is determined by the age and health of an animal.

Other considerations in successfully raising a baby animal include feeding methods, conspecific digestive enzymes (beneficial bacteria specific to an individual species), habitat enrichment, stimulation for elimination, and imprinting.

As you can see, raising baby wildlife is a science, and the animals (who are living, feeling creatures) deserve more than trial and error or guesses.

NUISANCE WILDLIFE

There are times when the animal found is not in danger but is in itself the problem.

As civilization spreads, we are encroaching more and more upon wild animal habitat. Animals either adapt or perish, and in today's world, many are adapting. An urban area is a wildlife mecca, and species thought to be strictly rural, such as the red fox, are becoming urbanized. As the human population increases, this cohabitation will become even more pronounced.

Animals are extremely opportunistic and will inhabit homes and backyards because the shelter and food is plentiful and life is easy. It may be enjoyable to watch a pair of squirrels playing and jumping acrobatically through the trees in your backyard. It is quite another thing when you've discovered that they are living in the walls of your home.

When faced with a nuisance wild animal in or near your home, first make sure that you are not causing the problem. Are you doing anything to attract the animal? Are you feeding one type of animal and have, unknowingly, opened up a buffet for all?

Bird feeders are often the cause of many uninvited wild animal guests. The food not only attracts squirrels that can climb the feeders, but it also falls to the ground, attracting ducks, geese, raccoons, bears, and rodents such as rats and mice.

Cat food put out for the neighborhood felines is a request for all the area skunks, raccoons, and opossums to come calling.

Before taking desperate measures to rid your property of nuisance animals, scrutinize your own behavior and that of your close neighbors to be sure you are not encouraging the problem. If you are, please discontinue the practice!

Bird Feeder Bandits

We often get complaints about two problem animals in regards to bird feeders: hawks and squirrels. First, let's talk about hawks.

When you put out bird food, you are attracting a large number and variety of songbirds to a small area. For the animals that prey upon songbirds, that means you've gathered together a vast variety of food for them and the chances of a successful hunt at this location are good.

There is only one way to stop a hawk from being a constant watchman over your yard—stop feeding the birds. You have to stop feeding for a period of several weeks until the hawk moves on to other hunting grounds. If the hawk lives and nests locally, you will need to stop feeding indefinitely.

Another way to deal with the situation is to look at it differently. If you put food out to attract the activity of wildlife to your yard, then you have been extremely successful. When you feed the birds, you feed *all* the birds, including the

hawks. Enjoy the opportunity to witness wildlife at its greatest. Life in the wild can be brutal, but that is the essence of nature.

Squirrels are frequent thieves of the bird feeder, emptying the contents quickly and even destroying feeders to get at the food. Squirrel-proof bird feeders do not always work and can be expensive.

One trick that often helps keep squirrels away is to lace the bird seed liberally with powdered red pepper. The taste is a deterrent for rodents, but the birds don't seem to even notice.

Birds Attacking Windows

A common songbird problem during nesting season is birds attacking windows. The culprit is usually a male bird, frequently a cardinal.

The cause is quite simple: This confused bird sees its reflection in the window and thinks it's a competitor male out to take over its nesting area. The bird becomes obsessed with chasing it off and consequently flying at its own reflection.

If this were a real bird and not a reflection, such behavior would quickly end with the weaker bird leaving the area. With a reflection, however, a bird is met with equal action, resulting in a stalemate. Its obsession can become so great that it never attracts a mate, never nests, and may injure or kill itself colliding with the window.

The cure to this problem is also quite simple: You must remove the reflection. The easiest way is to allow the windows to remain "dirty" because only clean windows reflect well. Reflection from a clean window can be eliminated by spraying with soapy or salty water and allowing it to dry. A more permanent solution is to install dark screening on the outside of the windows.

We've even heard stories of this behavior toward cars. Birds have been reported attacking side-view mirrors, windows, and shiny paint.

The same concept applies. Although you would not want to spray salty water on your car, consider putting the car in a garage or covering it while it's parked. A cloth draped over a mirror will eliminate the attractiveness of the mirror.

Birds that Fly at You

Another common problem during nesting season involves birds dive-bombing people as they enter and exit a doorway. Typically, the bird is nesting nearby and feels threatened by your presence. This activity usually occurs when there are eggs or hatchlings in the nest.

Try to determine what species of bird it is and the location of the nest. The species will give you an indication of where the nest is located and how long the nesting period lasts. Depending on the species, incubation is generally one to three weeks.

When the eggs hatch and the parents are busy gathering food for their hungry offspring, this activity may or may not cease.

If you can enter and exit by way of another door, that would be the simplest solution. If this is not possible, setting a visual barrier between the doorway and the nest—such as a dressing blind or sheet—may give the birds a feeling of security.

Woodpeckers Destroying Wooden Homes

Woodpeckers peck wood—that's what they do and why they are so named. The echo of rhythmic drumming on a country morning is a wonderful sound—unless the wood being drilled is part of your home. Woodpecker damage can be quite extensive and expensive, but it can be prevented.

When a woodpecker drums, it is actually looking for insects hiding under tree bark. If you have an insect infestation of the wood, these birds will alert you to the problem. An inspection by an exterminator may be in order.

If there are no insects but a bird seems determined to dismantle your home, bright yellow balloons hung on the side of the home usually will chase them away. Mylar balloons will hold up better in the weather, but you'll need to use a bright yellow color. Attach the balloon to the side or corner of your home with a one- to two-foot line, allowing the balloon to move with the breeze. You may need to hang one on each outside wall to protect the entire building. No one knows exactly why yellow balloons seem to work better than other colors; one theory is that they remind woodpeckers of owl eyes. Many pest control agencies even sell yellow balloons with a black dot on each side to resemble pupils. These can be expensive, however, and mylar balloons found in your local grocery store will work just as well.

Squirrels in Your Home

Squirrels living inside the walls of a house present a very dangerous situation. These destructive rodents can chew on wiring and have caused electrical house fires.

High-frequency sound emitters, mothballs, pepper sprays, and animal deterrents only work for a short time, if at all. Removing the housing and food source is the best way to prevent squirrel damage to your home.

Move bird feeders at least twenty feet from the house, promptly remove all outdoor pet foods, keep your barbeque clean (including the drip pan), and keep garbage in tightly closed metal cans.

Examine your home for entrance areas, and seal the area with half-inch hardware cloth (stainless steel mesh screening with half-inch spacing). Once squirrels get inside your home, the only real solution is to relocate them. Do not trap during the squirrels' nesting season as you may potentially separate a mother squirrel from her babies. You will then have a second wildlife emergency on your hands. Gray squirrels typically have two litters per year, one in the early spring and one in the late summer to fall. Early summer is often the best time to relocate squirrels.

Squirrels can be live-trapped out of the area either by you or a wildlife pest control person. Before attempting to trap squirrels yourself, contact the state wildlife agency where you live to be certain your can legally trap the animals. The contact numbers are located on page 126.

Traps can be purchased or rented from local hardware stores. Live traps for squirrels are about $5 \times 5 \times 18$ inches long with one door and $\frac{1}{2} \times 1$–inch wire spacing. Sizing is important—the wrong dimensions will not catch any squirrels, and overly large wire spacing can injure a squirrel.

Extra crunchy peanut butter is excellent bait for squirrels, as are a variety of shelled nuts. Bait and place the trap in the area where the squirrels generally run and check the trap several times each day, especially in the morning and the evening.

Once captured, drive the squirrel to a wilderness habitat with a large variety of nut-bearing trees (such as oak) at least five miles from your home. Be careful releasing squirrels, as they have long, sharp, curved teeth that can cause a serious puncture.

Raccoons in the Chimney or Attic

Raccoons can live in chimneys and attics for long periods without detection. The first sign is often the sound of babies that are a few weeks old.

Raccoons can be encouraged to leave a denning area such as a shed or attic by making their stay uncomfortable. They prefer a dark quiet location, so turn on the lights and turn up the music. Placing a loud radio in the attic and turning on bright lights will compel the mother to find a new location. It may take her a few days, but soon

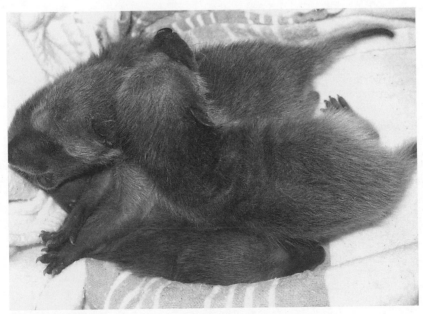

Newborn raccoons

she will move all the babies and vacate. Once she has left with the babies, seal off all entrance points to prevent further problems.

Raccoons in chimneys are a bit more difficult and require the installation of a chimney cap. Make sure there are no animals inside the chimney or they will be trapped and starve, or may even enter your home. Raccoons need to be live-trapped and relocated before a chimney cap is installed.

Raccoons can also be relocated by a professional urban wildlife pest control expert. Ask the company about the method of disposal. Some states require professionally trapped animals to be destroyed.

Rabbits in the Garden
Rabbits can easily be kept from eating gardens and tree bark by removing cover where they hide and installing fencing. Fencing to exclude rabbits needs to be at least two feet high and have a maximum of one-inch-square wire spacing.

Skunk Odor Neutralizer

> 1 quart of 3 percent hydrogen peroxide
> ¼ cup of baking soda
> 1 teaspoon of liquid soap

Mix ingredients only when needed and apply immediately to affected area. Massage into the area for about two minutes. Rinse with water.

Do not store the solution! If you put it into a capped container, it may explode!

Wildlife Repellent Recipe, from Carol Martino
This recipe works well for pesky mammals. The solution must be applied every two weeks and after it rains until the problem is resolved.

Ingredients:
> 1 whole Spanish onion
> 1 jalapeño pepper
> 1 tablespoon cayenne pepper
> 2 quarts of water

Directions:

Chop up the onion and the jalapeño pepper. Stir in the cayenne pepper. Boil mixture in two quarts of water for about twenty minutes. Let cool, then strain the water through cheesecloth. Using a garden sprayer, spray any area outside where wild animals or even neighborhood pets are being a nuisance.

This process may have to be carried out for a period of two weeks to ensure success.

The mixture is nontoxic and will not harm any animal, but it will succeed in keeping them away.

Chapter 8

ABOUT WILDLIFE REHABILITATION

Wildlife rehabilitation involves a network of individuals and organizations caring for injured, sick, and orphaned wild animals with the goal of releasing these animals back into their natural habitats. Wildlife rehabilitators have demonstrated a proficient knowledge of wildlife by passing both written and oral examinations, have met certain housing standards for species they are permitted to treat, attend continuing education classes, and work with a licensed veterinarian.

Wildlife rehabilitation is often the last hope for sick and injured animals.

Through rehabilitation, an animal is given the benefits of proper nutrition and husbandry as well as modern medical care including fluid and drug therapy, diagnostics, x-rays, and surgery. For animals that cannot survive in the wild, or who are beyond the ability to recover, rehabilitators offer a painless end to their suffering.

Individuals who unlawfully possess wildlife not only endanger the health and well-being of that animal, but also risk their own health, as well as the health of their family and pets. In addition to the physical injury a wild animal can inflict, wildlife carry diseases and parasites that can infect humans and domestic animals. Furthermore, animals that have been humanized pose a great threat to the people they encounter as well as to themselves.

By offering an alternative, wildlife rehabilitation provides the public with a humane, legal way of dealing with the wildlife in need that they encounter. The person who finds and rescues a wild animal is the first step in the process of returning an animal to its natural habitat, as well as in protecting the public health. From the moment you pick up an animal in distress, you become part of the network of individuals whose purpose is to give that animal a second chance at life.

WHY ARE THERE SO FEW REHABILITATORS?

Although we are a country that purports to love and protect our wildlife, there is *no* state or federal funding for wildlife rehabilitation. Governmental agencies heavily regulate the activity, but they do not support it.

Most wildlife rehabilitators don't get paid for their services, and they are responsible for raising the funds necessary to support their work. Many have outside employment to cover the cost of rehabilitation in addition to their own living expenses. It is difficult for any person to devote the time, space, and money to rehabilitate wildlife properly.

Those who dedicate their lives to the hundreds, even thousands, of animals that come through their doors each year do so because of a deep devotion to their charges.

FIND A LOCAL WILDLIFE REHABILITATOR

If you've been directed to this page, then you have a true wildlife emergency or need further advice from a wildlife rehabilitator.

I have attempted to supply as much information as possible to get you started, and all the web resources and contact numbers listed are current as of this book's publication date.

The entities I've listed on the following pages have been around a long time and are extremely helpful. You can also find other resources by doing an Internet search for "find a wildlife rehabilitator."

Wildlife rehabilitators do not generally advertise their services, and it is rare to find one listed in the Yellow Pages. Funds are usually limited, and the expense of advertising is a luxury most rehabilitators cannot afford.

Rehabilitators do, however, network with local veterinarians and animal shelters. A call to these places may yield information about a local rehabilitator.

Licensed wildlife rehabilitators are regulated by two governing bodies: the state fish and game or conservation department and, if they work with migratory birds, the U.S. Fish and Wildlife Service. These organizations can be found in the Blue Pages of your telephone directory. Also supplied on pages 126–129 is a list of government agencies and their contact numbers that is current as of publication.

Please keep in mind that you may have to make several phone calls before finding a rehabilitator close to you who may be able to help. Please be patient and persistent—that animal is relying on *you!*

Resources

WEB RESOURCES

Red Creek Wildlife Center
www.RedCreekWildlifeCenter.com
The official site for Red Creek supplies links and search features for locating wildlife rehabilitators.

The National Wildlife Rehabilitators Association
www.nwrawildlife.org
This association publishes up-to-date documents regarding state and federal agencies that regulate wildlife rehabilitation.

The Wildlife Rehabilitation Information Directory
www.tc.umn.edu/~devo0028/
Developed by Ronda DeVold and hosted by the University of Minnesota, this extensive wildlife rehabilitation resource lists contacts throughout the world. This valuable and exhaustive site also offers information and pictures relating to wildlife rehabilitation.

Wildlife International
www.wildlifeinternational.org
Wildlife International was built on a grant from the Humane Society of the United States and is maintained by the International Wildlife Rehabilitation Council (IWRC). It contains some suggestions for common wildlife issues and has a search option for rehabilitators.

GOVERNMENT AGENCIES

United States of America

STATE	STATE AGENCY	USFW REGIONAL OFFICE
Alabama	Div of Wildlife/Freshwater Fisheries 334-242-3467	Region 4 404-679-7049
Alaska	Dept of Fish & Game 907-465-4190	Region 7 907-786-3693
Arizona	Arizona Game & Fish Dept 602-942-3000	Region 2 505-248-7882
Arkansas	AR Game & Fish Comm 870-873-4302	Region 4 404-679-7049
California	CA Dept of Fish & Game 916-445-0411	Region 1 503-872-2715
Colorado	CDOW/Special Licensing 303-291-7227	Region 6 303-236-8171 x630
Connecticut	DEP Wildlife Div 860-424-3011	Region 5 413-253-8643
Delaware	Div of Fish & Wildlife 302-739-9912	Region 5 413-253-8643
Florida	Florida F&W Cons Comm 850-488-6253	Region 4 404-679-7049
Georgia	Georgia DNR–Wildlife Res Div 770-761-3044	Region 4 404-679-7049
Hawaii	HI Div of Forestry & Wildlife 808-587-0400	Region 1 503-872-2715
Idaho	Dept of Fish & Game 208-334-3700	Region 1 503-872-2715
Illinois	Dept of Natural Resources 217-782-6302	Region 3 612-713-5449
Indiana	DNR 317-233-6527	Region 3 612-713-5449
Iowa	IA DNR 515-281-5918	Region 3 612-713-5449

STATE	STATE AGENCY	USFW REGIONAL OFFICE
Kansas	KS Dept of Wildlife & Parks 620-672-5911	Region 6 303-236-8171 x630
Kentucky	KY Dept of Fish & Wildlife Resources 800-858-1549	Region 4 404-679-7049
Louisiana	LDWF Natural Heritage Program 225-765-2800	Region 4 404-679-7049
Maine	Dept of Inland Fish & Wildlife 207-287-8000	Region 5 413-253-8643
Maryland	DNR 410-260-8100	Region 5 413-253-8643
Massachusetts	Div of Fisheries & Wildlife 617-626-1500	Region 5 413-253-8643
Michigan	DNR 517-373-1263	Region 3 612-713-5449
Minnesota	DNR Nongame Wildlife Program 651-296-6157	Region 3 612-713-5449
Mississippi	Dept of Wildlife, Fish & Parks 601-354-7303 x109	Region 4 404-679-7049
Missouri	Dept of Conservation 573-751-4115	Region 3 612-713-5449
Montana	MT Fish, Wildlife & Parks 406-444-2612	Region 6 303-236-8171 x630
Nebraska	Nebraska Game & Parks Comm 402-471-0641	Region 6 303-236-8171 x630
Nevada	NV Dept of Wildlife 775-688-1500	Region 1 503-872-2715
New Hampshire	NH Fish & Game Dept 603-271-3127	Region 5 413-253-8643
New Jersey	NJ Div of Fish, Game & Wildlife 609-292-2965	Region 5 413-253-8643
New Mexico	NM Dept of Game & Fish 505-476-8000	Region 2 505-248-7882

STATE	STATE AGENCY	USFW REGIONAL OFFICE
New York	NYS Dept Env Con 518-402-8995	Region 5 413-253-8643
North Carolina	N.C. Wildlife Resources Comm 919-707-0060	Region 4 404-679-7049
North Dakota	ND Game & Fish Dept 701-328-6300	Region 6 303-236-8171 x630
Ohio	Wildlife Management 614-265-6300	Region 3 612-713-5449
Oklahoma	OK Wildlife Conservation 405-521-3719	Region 2 505-248-7882
Oregon	Oregon Fish & Wildlife 503-947-6312	Region 1 503-872-2715
Pennsylvania	PA Game Comm 717-783-8164	Region 5 413-253-8643
Rhode Island	Div of Fish & Wildlife 401-789-0281	Region 5 413-253-8643
South Carolina	South Carolina Dept of Natural Res 803-734-3886	Region 4 404-679-7049
South Dakota	Game, Fish & Parks 605-773-3381	Region 6 303-236-8171 x630
Tennessee	TWRA/Law Enforcement 615-781-6610	Region 4 404-679-7049
Texas	Nongame Permits 512-389-4800	Region 2 505-248-7882
Utah	DNR Div of Wildlife Res 801-538-4700	Region 6 303-236-8171 x630
Vermont	Agency Natural Resources 802-241-3727	Region 5 413-253-8643
Virgin Islands	Div of Fish & Wildlife 340-775-6762	
Virginia	VA Dept of Game & Inland Fisheries 804-367-1258	Region 5 413-253-8643

STATE	STATE AGENCY	USFW REGIONAL OFFICE
Washington	Dept of Fish & Wildlife 360-902-2267	Region 1 503-872-2715
West Virginia	Div Natural Resources 304-558-2771	Region 5 413-253-8643
Wisconsin	Dept of Natural Resources 608-266-2621	Region 3 612-713-5449
Wyoming	Game & Fish Dept 307-777-4600	Region 6 303-236-8171 x630

Canada

PROVINCE	PROVINCIAL AGENCY
Alberta	Minister of Environment #423, 10800-97 Ave Edmonton, AB T5K 2B6
British Columbia	Ministry of Sustainable Resources PO Box 9372 Stn Prougut Victoria, BC V8W 9M3
Manitoba	Manitoba Conservation 204-945-7465
Nova Scotia	Environmental Monitoring and Compliance (902) 424-2547
Ontario	Ministry of Natural Resources 705-755-1999
	Canadian Wildlife Service 519-472-5750
Quebec	Ministere Des Ressources Naturelles et De la Faune 418-627-8694
Saskatchewan	SE & RM – Fish & Wildlife Branch 306-787-6218

About the Author

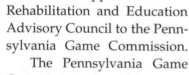

A Pennsylvania-licensed wildlife rehabilitator since 1991, Peggy Sue Hentz is the founder and director of Red Creek Wildlife Center, Inc.

She was elected to the board of directors of the Pennsylvania Association of Wildlife Rehabilitators (PAWR) in 2003 and currently serves as association president. In 2005, she was appointed to the Rehabilitation and Education Advisory Council to the Pennsylvania Game Commission.

The Pennsylvania Game Commission adopted her manual on wildlife capture and transport to set its new state guidelines for people permitted to respond to wildlife emergencies.

An accomplished public speaker, she has presented more than five hundred public programs on wildlife. She is also a regular presenter at many state and national wildlife rehabilitation conferences and teaches classes on wildlife capture and transportation.